Selling Outside the Square

Creative Ideas to Help YOU
Make More $ales to Millennials

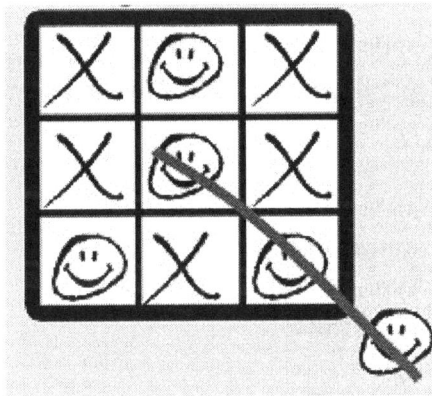

By Bob Boog

Author of *Real Estate Sales from Hell*

ths international publishing

Selling Outside the Square: Creative Ideas to Help YOU Make More Sales to Millennials

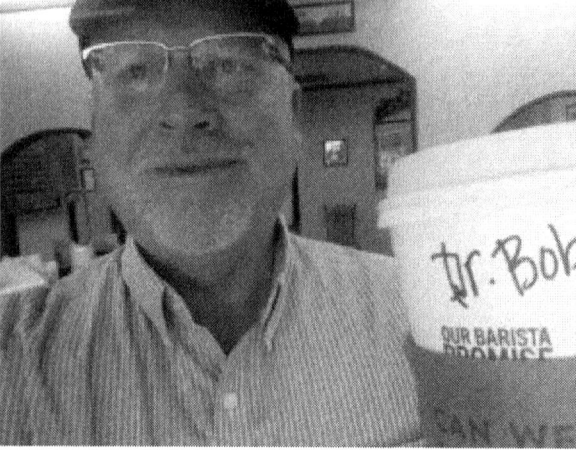

By Bob Boog

Book design cover art by: Robert Boog
© 2012 by Robert Boog, all rights reserved

Published in Santa Clarita, California by:
THS International Publishing
 23916 Lyons Avenue
Santa Clarita, Ca. 91321

ISBN: 978-0-9666130-7-0

First printing: November 2012
Printed in the United States of America

Acknowledgments

To Roxana,
Thank you for giving me space to make my dreams come true.

To my sons **Brandon and Kevin:** hoping that they will use the principles of this book to increase their future success and happiness.

Special thanks to my Dad and Mom, brothers and sisters, Jim and Jane Behan, Lyle & Geoff Olsen, Gary & Jackie Kipka, Mary Clark, Mike Change and my many friends, clients, customers & creditors living in Santa Clarita, CA.

Disclaimer

This book was diligently researched and compiled with the intent to provide information for persons wishing to learn about selling using creative selling techniques. Throughout the making of this book, every effort has been made to ensure the highest amount of accuracy and effectiveness for the techniques suggested by the author. The book may contain contextual as well as typographical mistakes and there may be hypertext links to products or services where the author may receive financial benefits or other forms of compensation from a service provider.

No information provided in this book constitutes a warranty of any kind; nor shall readers rely solely on any such information or advice. All content, products, and services are NOT to be considered as legal, medical, or professional advice and are to be used for personal use and information purposes only. This book makes no warranties or guarantees express or implied, as to the results provided by the strategies, techniques, and advice presented in this book. The publishers of this book expressly disclaim any liability arising from any strategies, techniques, and advice presented in this book.

The purpose of this book is to educate and guide. The author does not warrant that the information contained herein is free of omissions or errors and is fully complete.

Furthermore, the author shall not have responsibility or liability to any entity or person as a result of any damage or loss alleged to be caused or caused indirectly or directly by this book.

Contents

A Different Perspective   7

Selling Inside the Square Explained   244

Trigger #1: Give a Reason Why.   266

Trigger #2: Ask Statement-Questions   30

Trigger #3: Use Stories to Sell   323

Trigger #4: Deftly Answer Objections   411

Trigger #5: Use Curiosity   455

Trigger #6: Commitment & Consistency   48

Trigger #7: The Scarcity Principle   53

Trigger # 8: Social Proof   58

Trigger # 10: Authority   67

Trigger #11: Just Like Me!   74

Trigger #12: Tell the Truth!   80

Conclusion: Where to Go from Here?   85

Seven Creative Thinking Questions   99

Selling Outside the Square Humor   **114**

Six Laws for Selling Outside the Square   **116**

Helpful Resources   **118**

Other Books by Bob Boog   **118**

Index   **119**

A Different Perspective

There was once a wife who asked her husband, "Honey, could you please go shopping for me and buy one carton of milk and if they have avocados, get six?"

A short time later, the husband returned with six cartons of milk.

The wife asked him, "Why did you buy six cartons of milk?"

The husband replied, "Because they had avocados."

Obviously the wife assumed that the husband would bring one carton of milk and six avocados. Yet the husband had thought that she meant, "If they have avocados bring me back six cartons of milk."

Some women will probably read this and think, "Oh my God, that just proves how stupid some men can be."

While some men might reply, "What's the big deal? He did follow her directions, didn't he?"

Chalk it up to having different perspectives.

Likewise, my selling point of view might be different than yours. I have been involved in selling real estate "full-time" for over 30 years.

Some of you might be thinking, "Wow, that's a long time. I might learn something." Others might be not be so sure. In fact, you might be wondering, "Will this book be useful to me? After all, I don't plan on buying or selling real estate anytime soon – and I'm not a realtor."

For this reason, I appreciate that you are giving me a chance. After all, you may have made more sales than me. You are probably a ~~little~~ lot smarter than me too (after all, I do sell real estate.)

But during my time on this planet, I have made a number of observations that some folks have called **"interesting" or "unique"** More than one person has said to me, "Gee, I never considered **that before**."

And it wasn't just some floozy straggling out of the bar near my office who has said this. Even sober people have made this comment!

When I was a young boy, for example, watching *The Wizard of Oz* on TV was a big deal in our family. We would visit my grandmother to watch the movie at her home because she owned a color TV. **Half** of the movie was in color and that was a big deal back then.

Anyway, one time after watching this movie, I asked a simple question: *Why would the Wicked Witch of the West keep a bucket of water there in the kitchen with all those flying monkeys buzzing around? It doesn't make sense. One angry monkey could easily douse her and cause her to melt.*

"Thanks for ruining the movie," griped my older brother.

When I attended Catholic school, I asked a dumb question about the Bible that stunned many fellow students when I uttered it. Even my teacher said she had never considered it before. I asked my teacher: *"Why did God create man twice?"*

She said, "What do you mean?"

"Well, in Chapter One of the Bible," I explained, "It reads, 'God created man in His own image, let them have dominion over the fish of the sea, man and woman created he them.' Then God rested on the seventh day."

"Yes," she said. "What is your point?"

"In Chapter Two," I continued, "God makes Adam and Eve. So why did God create man twice? He had already created man in Chapter One on the sixth day, therefore it doesn't make sense to do it again in Chapter Two, does it?"

My teacher answered with, "I never really thought of that. Class, let's move on to social studies."

"Thanks for ruining my creation beliefs," I can almost hear someone mutter.

When I first started selling real estate, I was taught to show a buyer three homes with the last one being the best one. Then I was supposed to bring the buyers back to the office and have a lender talk to them about financing the purchase.

So I asked this dumb question, "What if the buyer doesn't qualify for the loan?" No problem. I was told that this would **NEVER** happen.

I was told that a buyer would **ALWAYS** find the money, or borrow it from a wealthy relative. Fast forward to the day when my buyers didn't qualify. They did NOT have any solvent relatives either.

After that experience, before I showed homes to a buyer, I had a lender run their credit and/or get them preapproved for their financing first. Then, knowing that I had a qualified customer, rather than speeding back to the office, I would stop at a ~~fancy, upscale~~ restaurant (Umm, McDonald's) where I would buy them McDonald's special brew of ultra-hot coffee.

They would blow on the coffee and chit-chat while their kids played on the playground and I would dutifully write up the purchase contract for their new home.

I started doing this some 28+ years ago and I sold a number of homes this way.

It's funny too because nowadays almost every real estate agent I know will prequalify their clients before showing them a property.

Yet back then, some people told me that I was crazy. I could lose good customers by making them get them prequalified first. I was "pushing the envelope" and "thinking outside the box." My how times have changed!

What you do may be similar to selling real estate or it may be poles apart and I respect that. And because your time is valuable, I want you to know why you should continue reading this book and what makes it different.

Myself, I enjoy sales books that teach new techniques about leading someone to make a purchasing decision. I am also a sucker for books that help motivate me to make more sales. I even have a weakness for books on selling that have "rich" or "millionaire" in their titles. I study the art of persuasion because I want to know how to sell better, but one day I asked myself a dumb question: **What causes a buyer to make a purchase in the first place?**

Is there a psychological reason? If so, can I use it to better motivate him or her to purchase a product? After all, most folks have heard of Ivan Pavlov and how he conditioned his dogs to respond to the ringing of a bell. When I researched why human beings purchase things, I discovered that researchers believe that most people have been conditioned to respond to certain buying cues. They will let down their guard and buy more readily when they receive certain signals called **psychological triggers**.

The 12 psychological triggers in this book are not my creation, but they are backed with scientific data and if you give it a chance, this book may help you to better lead your average customer towards making a purchase.

But what if you already know about these cues or triggers? Then a review on them won't kill you either.

After all, when you truly understand *why* something works it helps to internalize the idea better, doesn't it?

Can I guarantee 100% that the ideas presented here in this book will work wonders for you all of the time? **No**. That would not be truthful. My goal is to simply help you *increase your odds* for making more sales.

Also, I don't claim to be the sharpest knife in the drawer either (after all I am a realtor) therefore you may discover things that I have missed.

This book is written to help you bridge a gap of knowledge that you may not have considered before. Perhaps the creative problem solving section at the back of this book will help you avoid a predicament or answer a conundrum.

In fact, just skimming the creative answers raised by the questions may light a fire under your feet or help you to create a new and exciting product. It is my privilege to share this information with you too.

Now, this book is titled "Selling *Outside* the Square" but what if you are unfamiliar with that term? In other words, how can I sell "*outside*" the square if I don't even know what selling "*inside*" the square means? What if I don't even know what the square represents?

Good points, so in this book, I am going to first explain what I mean by the square. Then we'll move on to using the twelve psychological "triggers."

I'll also pepper the triggers with additional thoughts on how they might be used with the average American customer too. So if you are ready to get started, please turn the page!

For those who may have different versions of the Bible these first two verses below are from Chapter One of the King James Bible.

> 27 So God created man in his own image, in the image of God created he him; male and female created he them.
> 28 And God blessed them, and God said unto them, Be fruitful, and multiply, and replenish the earth, and subdue it; and have dominion over the fish of the sea, and over the fowl of the air, and over every living thing that moveth

> 7 And the LORD God formed man of the dust of the ground, and breathed into his nostrils the breath of life; and man became a living soul.
> 8 ¶ And the LORD God planted a garden eastward in Eden; and there he put the man whom he had formed.

And verses 7 and 8 are from Chapter Two.

Defining the Square

Have you ever heard the phrase "think outside of the box"? I realize that it's a cliché to say, "Think outside of the box," but there, I said it.

Note to reader: as soon as you utter a phrase like, "Let's think outside of the box," someone else will invariably pipe up and ask, "How did you get yourself into the box in the first place?"

So let's get one thing straight: the title of this book is "Think Outside The Square."

A square is defined as "a plane figure having four equal sides and four right angles." But the term "square" can refer to an "old-fashioned" person too. Think back to the days of Austin Powers. The people who were NOT hip back then were called "squares." "Don't be such a square, baby," as Austin Powers might say.

So when we talk about first defining the square, I want you to think about people. In particular: I want you to consider the values and beliefs of the average customer nowadays.

Have you ever considered who the average customer is these days? What is his or her focus?

What values and beliefs does this buyer hold dear? What is her inner mantra?

Does he believe, for example, that respect for others is important? Or is it more important to be respected by others?

When we talk about selling it's helpful to define your customer first before guessing about them or what they might want.

Then, once we know their motivation, or the motivation of the decision maker, we can figure out how to best market to them. So in this book, **I now hereby declare that every person in America is a square. And all the squares can fit inside of a big generational square too**. Here's what I mean. Let's arrange every person in America living today by his or her date of birth. When we do this, the top part of the square comprises The Greatest Generation. These folks were born prior to 1946. The next square would be for people born from 1946-1966 commonly known as the Baby-boomers. The next square would be for those folks born from 1966 – 1986, often called Generation X.

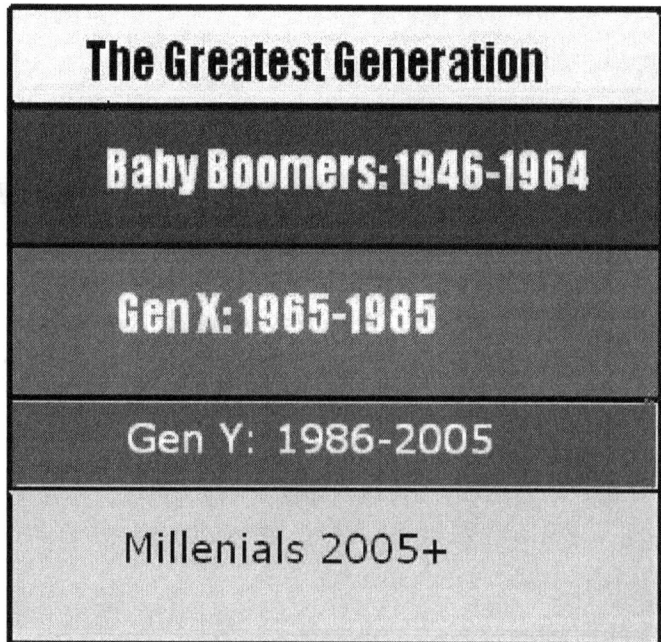

The Greatest Generation
Baby Boomers: 1946-1964
Gen X: 1965-1985
Gen Y: 1986-2005
Millenials 2005+

And next are the people of Generation Y, who were born after 1986.

Then our final square represents the Millennials: people born after 2005.

So everybody in America can fit into one of these squares – though admittedly, they do look more like rectangles.

[Please note: experts who study and research generations might disagree with my names/dates.]

But this is my book and I subscribe to the KISS principle, (Keep it Simple, Sweetie). Therefore, I hereby proclaim that only three generations exist: The Greatest Generation, Baby Boomers and the Me Generation.

(Nowadays, because Me Generation people are often called Millennials. I will also refer to them as either Millennials, Gen-Me or GenMe'ers.)

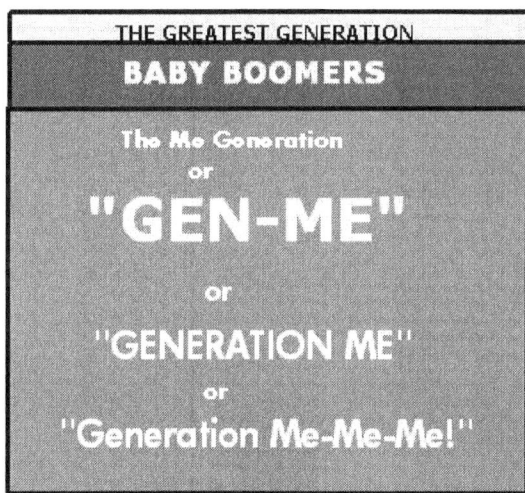

THE GREATEST GENERATION

BABY BOOMERS

The Me Generation
or
"GEN-ME"
or
"GENERATION ME"
or
"Generation Me-Me-Me!"

Once you look around, it's easy to see that Baby Boomers and The Greatest Generation have shrunk in size and are no longer the biggest advertising targets on earth. (Unless, that is, you sell life insurance and retirement planning.) In fact, Baby Boomers and the Greatest

Generation are now seen as "less desirable" to many advertisers because all the folks in these squares will be retiring soon or have already retired. Some might even be living in convalescent homes with one foot in that big square up in the sky. The point is: retired folks often live on fixed incomes and are not well-known for freely or carelessly spending their money.

I believe that many salespeople and politicians have failed to grasp that their target audience has changed. Unless, of course you specifically are targeting older people. The average American buyer is a Gen Me buyer.

> ## The majority of buyers now belong to "Generation Me"
> ### Born in 1969+

Some of you might be thinking, "What's the big deal? I know what Millennials think and believe. I know what they value." But do you?

See, I am not going to make that assumption. I want to know a little bit more about them. So I am going to rummage through their writings to learn what they are about. By the way, if you think this is all a bunch of Malarkey, I am not making this up. The credit for this information goes to Dr. Jean M. Twenge Ph.D. from San Diego State University.

In her book, *Generation Me*, author Jean M. Twenge Ph.D. used scientific research to compare and study people born after 1968 to the ones that came before it. Twenge compiled information that was collected in questionnaires filled out in the 1950s, 1960s, and 1970s and compared them to GenMe data. She noticed how the results and attitudes of people born in the 1980s and 1990s were much different than earlier attitudes. This helped her to arrive at her thesis statement about Millennials' beliefs, values, feelings, traits and attitudes. Here are some of her findings. Allow me to share them with you.

What to Know About the Me Generation

- ✓ GenMe is an entitled group who has been told from the time they could crawl, **"If you believe in yourself, then you can achieve anything."**

- ✓ The Millennial mantra is, **"You are special; you are important; being different is good; you first must love yourself before you love others."**

- ✓ GenMe believes that **people should respect themselves first, more so than they respect social rules or others.** The personality traits of these GenMe'ers emphasize a high degree of **individualism.**

Millennial Beliefs about the World

- Don't feel restricted by rules. Curse freely but don't conform. Be honest with the other person, even if the truth hurts the other person.

- There are no dress codes in life so wear tennis shoes and sandals and odd-looking clothing wherever and whenever you want – even to the White House – which some Millennials have done. (Some have worn flip-flops to the White House.)

- Tattoos, body art, and piercing are a form of GenMe self-expression. "The individual has always come first and feeling good about oneself is a primary virtue."

According to Twenge (who is a Millennial herself) "We speak the language of "the self" as our native tongue. So much of the 'common sense' advice that's given includes variations on the "self." Here are some examples:

- Worried about being in a social situation? **Be yourself.**

- Concerned about your performance? **Believe in yourself**

- Should you get the nose ring? **Yes, express yourself**.

- Want to get married? **You have to love yourself first before you can love someone else.**

- Should you express your own opinion? **Yes, express yourself**.

What Millennials Value

Self-image is very important to the Me Generation. They have been raised watching TV, videos, DVDs, and even YouTube. They have been photographed and videotaped by parents, family, friends, and relatives. They know the importance of looking good on camera in case they ever make it big one day. Many think they will strike it rich and become famous – just because they believe it. Nose jobs, breast implants, face-lifts, Botox, eyebrow waxing, going to the gym often, all of these are part of the idea that looking good means feeling good and feeling good makes us happy.

Many Millennials have an **extended adolescence** –they don't want to grow up.

Many Millennials have come from divorced households.

Many secretly crave success and fame quickly.

Many just crave stability and a father figure.

Generalized Religious Values

Many of the churches that have grown in membership promote a personalized form of religion with a strong Father figure. Example, Rick Warren of *The Purpose Driven Life* writes, "Accept yourself. Our Father (God) accepts us unconditionally. So instead of trying to do and say all the right things to make God love you, all you have to do is realize he loves you already and love him back."

Personal faith guarantees acceptance into heaven, so even if you're a murderer, you will be saved if Jesus is your Lord and Saviour.

Generalized Personality Traits

Weaned on television, Millennials like **visual advertising**.

They consider themselves individuals and fear "group-think." They compare groups to **zombies:** people who can't think for themselves.

GenMe'ers are computer literate and like things fast and easy.

They will boldly wear clothes that don't match. They are highly materialistic, yet have unrealistic expectations.

Many GenMe'ers have never lived in a world where video games, cell phones, Internet, emails and texting did not exist.

Generalized Feelings of Millennials

- ✓ Many Millennials worry a lot – after all, over half have seen their parents divorce, or don't know their father.
- ✓ Women worry about relationships, they use online dating services, and marry later in life.
- ✓ They often feel anger, sadness, pain, confusion and uncertainty with family issues.
- ✓ Some have a victim mentality and make excuses when things don't go "my" way.
- ✓ Millennials often blame everyone else for their own failures.
- ✓ "I am not at fault; someone else did it or made me do it."
- ✓ The flip side of self-freedom and only putting yourself first though, is loneliness.

✓ Millennials lack a feeling of community so they will look to create one through Facebook, Twitter, and other social media outlets.

Millennials and Politics

Politicians can't be trusted: look at Iran Contra, Clinton-Lewinski, and the search for weapons of mass destruction in Iraq. GenMe'ers favour politicians who look most like them or act like them. They ask themselves, "How can this politician best help me?" Politicians have to consider that with Millennials, it's okay for women to have babies without marrying the fathers. Gays and lesbians aren't willing anymore to stay hidden in the closet. Latinos and Asian Americans are staking their claim to a growing slice of the American pie.

Want to bet on who I think will win the 2012 election between President Obama and his challenger? I believe that President Obama will win re-election in 2012 hands-down, simply because his views are more consistent with the current GenMe electorate. What about the 2016 election? We'll talk about that later in this book.

What This All Means to Salespeople

Some marketers have already figured out that self is important to GenMe'ers and market in this direction. Prudential Life Insurance, for example, used to have a motto: "Get a piece of the rock." It now has a more individualistic motto: **"Be Your Own Rock."**

The U.S. Army's motto: "Be all you can be" is now Be an **"Army of One."**

From Wikipedia and Other Internet Sources

- ➢ "Millennials date cautiously. They don't feel that a traditional marriage is as important as loving one another. It's okay to remain single or for hetero as well as same-sex couples to live together."
- ➢ "Generation Me has survived a hurried childhood of divorce, latchkeys, space shuttle explosions (primarily in the United States), open classrooms, widespread political corruption, inflation and recession, devil-child movies, and a shift from "G" to "R" ratings."
- ➢ "Technology-wise the 'creation' and spreading of the internet has rendered face-to-face communication secondary. Books are now beside the point. Near-infinite knowledge is available on hand 24/7 and for Millennials; tech-related jobs are a hot commodity."
- ➢ "In jobs, GenMe'ers embrace risk and prefer free agency to loyal corporatism. Politically, they lean toward pragmatism and non-affiliation and libertarianism. Sometimes criticized as "slackers", they nevertheless were widely credited with a new growth of entrepreneurship and the resulting dot-com boom."
- ➢ "Millennials just love stuff. They love celebrities. They love technology. They love brand names. They're happy to do whatever advertising tells them to do. So what if they can't manage to read anything longer than an instant message? "
- ➢ "Not true. We grew up with courses that dissected the media and advertising. Millennials are even MORE aware of what's going on. "

Final Thoughts about Millennials:

Not every GenMe person owns several tattoos and a body piercing, or comes from a broken family. This is a very generalized view of things. If you belong to Generation Me or are a Millennial salesperson you are free to totally disagree with my assessment.

In addition, nowadays things change quickly too. **On the Internet, what exists today will probably exist differently tomorrow.** Rather than argue about it, let's say that Millennials ways are often random, ambiguous, and contradictory.

Like it or not I believe the Me Generation's individualistic ways have now become a part of American culture too. This is how the average customer views the world. Knowing this, how can we craft our sales message to motivate GenMe buyers? Read on! "

"

Selling Inside the Square Explained

Now that we have a general idea about "the GenMe square" and how they are often random, ambiguous and contradictory, selling "inside" the square to them should be a cinch, right? No, not really but hopefully it may help to open your eyes or to fine-tune your sales message.

By the way, the conventional ways of selling that I am about to cover should not be looked at in a pejorative sense. It is crucial for salespeople to understand how most people are normally persuaded because that is the art of sales: to convince a prospect or buyer to **take some kind of action**.

At the same time, though, we want to be cognizant of the *Great-Grandma Effect* when it arises. There is probably a scientific name for this effect but it just means that many of us do things a certain way without asking why. And when asked why, someone will often answer, "Because that's the way we've always done it." Period.

There is a story about a young woman who was going to bake a ham for Christmas. Her mother explained that to properly cook it, the daughter needed to carve one inch off the ham on all sides before she put it into the pan to roast it in the oven.

The young woman asked her mother, "Why?" and her mother answered, "I don't know. It's just the way my Great-Grandma did it and everyone likes it this way."

Well it just so happened that Great-Grandma stopped by later that afternoon, so the girl asked her directly, "Why did you shave one inch off the ham before baking it?" Great Grandma answered, "Oh, I did that so the ham would fit into my square pan."

The point of the story is that there may be a good reason for doing things a certain way, because sometimes the old ways are the best ways. However, advances in technology may have made things easier or obsolete too, so don't be afraid to examine and review your sales systems.

Finally, like all buyers, Millennials will want to know what your product or service can do for them. **They also want to feel like you understand them and their pain; that your product or service will truly help remedy what ails them. They also want to trust you.**

The good news is that the twelve psychological triggers involved in "selling inside the square" will help you do these things, but it's like a man who couldn't fix his computer, and paid an expert big money to repair it.

When the specialist got the computer running in seconds, the man complained because all the expert did was unplug the mouse and hook it back in to the computer. "You didn't pay me for the time today," said the professional, "You paid me for all the time it took me to learn what I needed to do."

Likewise, sometimes it's also a matter of knowing when and where to use this information about psychological triggers. Most people, not all, will let their guard down when they are used and will buy things more readily. Tweak them slightly when needed to better fit your own customer's needs. Turn the page to read about Trigger#1.

Trigger #1: Give a Reason Why.

Telling people the reason why you need them to do something often influences them in a very powerful way. Humans are naturally curious and need to know why they should buy what you are selling before they'll purchase it. In his book, *"Influence, the Psychology of Persuasion,"* author Robert Cialdini Ph.D. writes about an experiment performed by Ellen Langer of Harvard. The experiment consisted of twelve or more average humans waiting in line to use a library copy machine. The experimenter would ask to cut in line, and then recorded the reaction of the person waiting next in line to see how he or she would react.

When the experimenter asked, "May I cut in front of you to use the Xerox machine?" the request was granted 60% of the time. Not bad. But watch what happened when the experimenter would give a reason why. "Excuse me, I have five pages," he would explain. "May I cut in line to use the Xerox machine because I'm in a rush?" Guess what percentage of people allowed the experimenter to cut in line? Answer: 94%. In fact, **the percentage was still 93%** when the experimenter asked, "Excuse me, may I cut in front of you to use the Xerox machine because I need to make some copies?"

I want you to stop.

Think about that for just a second. The requester asked, "May I cut in front of you to use the Xerox machine, because I need to make some copies?"

Let me ask you a question. What percentage of library-card-carrying citizens who were patiently standing in line was there to make copies?

The answer is 100%.

So the people waiting in line didn't care about the reason given, did they? No. They just heard the word "because," and assumed that the experimenter must have had a good reason! Langer concluded that the word "because" is a powerful motivator in persuasion, advertising and in sales. Interesting, isn't it?

Give people a reason "why" and you can move mountains.

Selling Outside the Square Perspective 1

As seen in this first trigger, your prospects need to have a compelling reason why they should buy from you. So the next time you watch a TV commercial, ask yourself: does this commercial succeed in offering a visual "reason why" I should buy the product?

So, if you are involved in "belly-to-belly" sales, you may find it wise to have three fixed reasons in your mind as to why a GenMe customer should buy from you. Remember that a GenMe customer likes to receive information quickly and not hear a bunch of gobbly--gook.

Therefore, keep your eyes peeled on technological ways to help deliver products, services and information faster.

In real estate sales, for example, an agent can set up a text message system that instantly sends listing information to prospective buyers via their cell phones using text messages.

This service is called "text info to clients".

It's handy because many Gen Me prospects don't carry around a pen, but most do clutch a cell phone. The prospect sends a text to the message on a sign and automatically receives a text back with a link to a mobile website where there are pictures and information on the subject property! (It even saves trees! Could your business benefit from using this kind of instant texting service?

Idea #1: Come up with three unique, compelling reasons why a GenMe prospect should purchase your product or service and write them down. Create a mnemonic spelling of these reasons. Repeat them to make them memorable. Doing so will give you added confidence especially when on a job interview.

For example: **DURP**: "Because our product is **D**urable, **U**nique, and **R**easonably **P**riced."

Knowing what's different or unique about your product or service will help you sell it better because people will think that you are on the ball and know what you're doing. When you can intelligently define the features and benefits of something, you won't come off sounding like a nincompoop. Plus you can usually become more enthusiastic about a product's benefits.

Idea #2: Keep an online or offline journal. I think it helps to spend a few moments each day and document your feelings, success stories and ideas. Use paper or Google docs.

Also, every religion out there says, "You will receive if you ask," so in your journal, don't be afraid to ask. Solicit the universe, God, Mother Nature or Spirit to help guide you. Then Listen.

Spend time in quiet meditation just listening. Sometimes a daily exercise of "automatic writing" after asking for daily guidance helps. Automatic writing means that you jot down whatever first comes to your mind.

Idea #3: Write down goals, but start small. Stay focused. More important, **remind yourself of the benefits you will receive** when you achieve your goals.

Practice delaying gratification until you have accomplished your work. For example: "Today after I make 50 sales calls I will treat myself to an all-you-can-eat sushi luncheon, or "after I close five sales by December 31, I will take my family on a Hawaiian vacation."

The daily contemplation of positives and rewards help to motivate action, which often helps to bring about a boost in sales!

Trigger #2: Ask Statement-Questions

Legendary sales trainer and *Selling for Dummies* author Tom Hopkins has often stated, **"When I make a statement of fact, people may doubt me. But if I ask a question and when answering, they make the statement of fact, people tend to believe me."**

This is an example of an inside the square technique that I call using a statement-question. To ask a statement-question, you simply add a question to the end of any statement or observation by adding words like, isn't it? Doesn't it? Wasn't it? Wouldn't it? Couldn't it? Shouldn't it? Don't you agree? Can't you? Won't you?

People from England seem to utter them all the time, ever notice that? They are always ending sentences with questions, aren't they?

Using statement-questions, a salesperson can help lead a prospect towards making a purchase, can't they? Asking a statement-question is easy to do, isn't it? Too many statement-questions can get irritating after a while, don't you agree?

Enough already!

Selling Outside the Square Perspective 2

Something I discovered when asking statement-questions is that if I could be **MORE** specific about a particular item, I would be seen as being more believable.

So instead of saying, "This living room is spacious, isn't it?" I would blurt out a more specific observation like, "Wow, that's a beautiful corner fireplace, isn't it?" or "The double-paned windows do add a nice touch to this room, don't you agree?"

"I didn't even notice they were double-paned."

Being specific is not limited to selling real estate. Specificity can aid anyone in persuasion because it adds to the believability factor. For example, "If I were to say, 'I sound like Willie Nelson when I sing." In your mind, you might have a good idea of what I think I sound like. But now my wife chimes in. She says, "Yeah right. **Bob sounds like a drunken Bob Dylan insisting that he's still okay to drive.**" Notice how that extra specificity helps? It's less namby-pamby. You get a **MUCH** better idea of how I sound!

Television commercials often use specifics to help demonstrate benefits. "Four out of five dentists recommend this gum for patients who chew gum."

Four out of five sounds more precise than "80%, doesn't it?

Yet if you do the math, **they are both the same**, (5 goes into .40 = 80%).

So when thinking of outside the square reasons, try to add a specific benefit along with the statement question. "Our soap is 99 percent pure, and smells amazing, doesn't it?" (99 per cent pure sounds more specific than 100% pure, don't you agree?)

Because most Millennials are skeptical about salespeople, use photographs, graphs, screenshots, and videos to provide proof of a specific benefit or feature.

The website, http://www.Screenr.com allows you to make a free video screenshot. It captures your cursor clicking on a particular website. Can providing video evidence that a buyer can click your website to download a product help your business? Possibly.

When using statement questions, don't be afraid to use pictures, present surveys or provide statistics too. One salesperson claimed that his three-minute video demonstrated the benefits of his product better than a presentation folder that his CPA had prepared. He said that the CPA had filled an impressive presentation folder with financial data including graphs that showed a measurable ROI (return on investment).

His video only revealed personal perks that the CPA's folder couldn't: he and his investors would be using a personal jet to fly to a Vegas Casino for a corporate meeting. He showed me pictures of him standing near his airplane. The takeaway is that a picture, video and graph along with a statement question can be worth 1,000 words and greatly increases your believability to a GenMe buyer. It may take a little more digging or research to create these items, but it's worth it. What happens in Vegas stays in Vegas, right?

Trigger #3: Use Stories to Sell

People love stories.
From ancient times to current day, a good story can hold a listener spellbound. Stories help to command attention and work almost like magic to influence and persuade people. Why do stories work so well? A good story plants a flag in the listener's brain and helps make a connection. In addition, stories help to let down people's barriers. After all, you're not going to give them a "sales pitch" you are just going to tell them a story, right?

But usually after telling the story you will share a connection to one of the benefits of your product or service and/or why it's important to take action today, rather than waiting. It's also important to **tell positive stories**, rather than negative ones, because an outcome of the story reflects how the listener views the person who tells it.

A study done at Ohio State University investigated negative stories told by people, and afterwards the participants were asked to relate the personality of the speaker.

Even though it was obvious the speaker was talking about or criticizing someone else, those same negative traits were attributed to the speaker when the listeners later filled out questionnaires! **So stay away from negative stories**. Here are three examples of using stories to sell:

Stories for Selling: The Wise Man Story

This first story can be very dramatic – especially if the speaker uses effective hand gestures while telling it.

There was once a man named MON who was believed to be the wisest man in all of India. The boys in the town didn't think that Mon looked that smart, so one of them decided to test him. He took a small bird and put it in his hands and asked the wise man, "Mon, is the bird in my hands alive or dead?" Now if the wise man answered that the bird was dead, the boy would open his hands and the bird would fly away freely.
But if the wise man answered that the bird was alive, the boy would take his hands **and crush the bird**. Holding the bird in his hands, the boy approached Mon and asked, "Wise man, is the bird in my hands alive or is it dead?" Mon looked at the boy and paused before he answered, "That decision, my child, lies in your hands."

The point of this story is realized when the salesperson says:

"Similarly, the decision to change your future lies in your hands."
"Similarly, the decision to believe in God lies in your hands."
"Similarly, the decision to protect your family from a financial catastrophe lies in your hands."

Do you see how this story can be used in sales by Amway salespeople, preachers, or insurance salespeople? It conveys the idea that an immediate, personal decision needs to be made.

Stories for Selling. The Mountain Story

This second story can be used when launching a product or service. It is a good story because it makes the prospect consider the pain involved.

There was once a man named Jim who as a boy read about one of the tallest mountains in the world and he told himself, "One day, I am going to climb that mountain." Twenty years passed, and Jim still hadn't achieved his goal – mainly because he discovered that he would need to learn how to rappel down the dangerous rocks that were at the top of the mountain. But he was so determined to climb the mountain that he quit his job and took up jogging in order to lose weight and get into top shape.

Jim purchased the best equipment, took rock-climbing classes and went on training hikes. Finally, one day Jim started his adventure. It took him three long weeks to climb the mountain, and at times he had to sleep at night dangling over an incredibly steep and dangerous cliff face. When he finally arrived at the top, he raised his arm in jubilation, but stopped because he heard a noise. Jim turned around and to his great surprise discovered that a helicopter had landed and off-loaded some skiers who jumped out and started skiing quickly down the mountain.

Similarly, ladies and gentlemen, **our new training course** offers students a rare opportunity. Now like the skiers on the mountain, anyone- even a beginner can take a short cut to success and avoid the pitfalls, dangers and sleepless nights as a result of doing it yourself. You will leapfrog over your competition.

This is a rather long story but it plants an indelible image in one's mind of the pain involved when someone takes on a task alone. The story then contrasts that pain by using a modern shortcut to success: a helicopter. Using contrast is a good tactic in storytelling.

Stories for Selling. The Email Letter Story

The next story was sent to me in an email I sent myself but it can be effective in offline sales as well because it sounds personal and offers specific benefits.

Dear [First Name], I recently stumbled upon something unusual, and as a valued subscriber, I wanted you to know about it.

A few months ago, I met a man named Bob Boog at a party. Bob is an author, a real estate broker and has made some observations that have helped people rank higher on Google and other search engines. He graciously offered his material to me and asked me to review it.

I politely smiled and thanked him, but I knew that I wouldn't get to it soon. (You should see my reading desk – it's piled high with material and I'm a fast reader, lol!)

But as luck would have it, my computer crashed and with nothing else to do, I decided to do some "light" reading.

Honestly, I can't remember a time when I started reading a book that I couldn't put down! Bob's manuscript, *Selling Outside the Square* combines scientific research on why people buy things, important information about today's Millennial buyers and tips for creative problem solving! The creative problem solving material is worth double the price of the book alone, but in addition, the book offers humor, has lots of stories, is fun to read, and presents useful tips on how to sell things in today's market.

Do yourself a favor and check it out here at this link.

You will be glad you did!

Sincerely,
 Bob

The beauty of this last story is that it refers to benefits that I might receive from purchasing this great book mentioned in the story.

What are its benefits? This book offers scientific research on why people buy things, has information about today's GenMe buyers and creative problem solving tips. It's an enjoyable read, plus the book offers humor, stories and I'll also learn about selling in today's market too.

Wow, I've managed to ~~shamelessly~~ plug my own book within my book!

Selling Outside the Square Perspective 3

Do you see how a story can help position the product or service? When you see an ad for a book or a sales-training course, you know that somebody is trying to sell you something. Yet most people get so wrapped up in listening to the "wise man" story that their minds' defenses about advertising have been lowered. The reality is that a salesperson is still going to make a call to action at the end of the story. Make sure your reader or listener understands this point. A story without a point is like telling a joke without a punch line.

But look at story #3. Bob uses a personal tone and writes passionately like he is your Facebook friend not an old fuddy-duddy. Adding the lol, helped to do that, didn't it? Lol = laughing out loud.

Having the greatest story in the world means nothing, however, unless your prospect hears about it or gets to read about it, so here are some more observations I've made.

Many snail-mail letters never get opened. So if you're writing a story and putting it in an envelope and mailing it, hoping it will be read, good luck. GenMe people are about as eager to open letters with computerized labels as opening a summons from the IRS.

So if you're going to snail-mail, I find it's more effective to use a blue-ink pen and handwrite the names and addresses on the envelopes.

(Outsource the handwriting job to your niece or fave senior citizen.) Not very efficient, but effective. Over-sized envelopes work well too but remember that the cost to mail over-sized letters is double.

Another effective strategy is to **send a lumpy package.** Wrap up a penny in bubble wrap and include it in your envelope with a witty little saying. "A penny for your thoughts." It may cost an extra penny, but lumpy letters often get opened. Not 100% but it improves your odds. It's like using this technique for getting into a housing tract with a security gate. Just dial any name on the list of homeowners, buzz their number and when the homeowner answers just say the magic word: U-P-S.

What about sending emails to Millennial customers? You will want the email to be opened and one way to do so is to employ the use of a "cliff-hanger." A cliffhanger is a suspenseful situation found at the end of most reality TV programs. For example, which singer on *American Idol* this week didn't make the cut? We'll find out, right after this lengthy commercial break. Which maverick will leave *Survivor*? The suspense of not knowing who will leave the reality show keeps viewers glued to their TV sets.

Likewise, when sending an email to a Millennial prospect, employ a **cliffhanger** in the subject line. The email has to be opened to discover the answer. Here's an example:
- Subject: What weird little secret are women using to lose weight? Find out inside!
- Subject: What's the fastest growing local website? (Note: it's NOT what you think!)
- Subject: Who just checked out your background? Open now to find out!

Notice how the subject lines almost force a reader to open the rest of the email?

One of the biggest challenges in sales, however, is to ascertain that the message has been received. In other words, if I don't receive a response from either my snail mail letter or my email, I might pick up the telephone and call the GenMe prospect to see if she got it. Or I could text her. If it's urgent, I might possibly leave an over-sized business card at her office.

When marketing to the Millennial population, an email with a link to an "app" or application is good to use too, because an app allows an individualistic GenMe'er the freedom to download things by himself and then tell his goombah, amigo or kindred spirit about it too. Most businesses build their reputations on satisfied, repeat customers, so give the populace what they like. Word of mouth really works, especially online.

The "no" you hear today might actually mean, "Not right now."

To learn more about handling an objection, turn the page!

Trigger #4: Deftly Answer Objections

Many salespeople take an ostrich approach to handling objections. They think that if they bury their head in the sand and keep silent about a possible objection, their prospect won't even be thinking of it. Not true. Sometimes it's wise just to float a possible objection to the surface to see if it is a true deal-breaker or not.

In fact, some companies will openly advertise the defects of their products. "These shirts are so frickin' ugly, we gotta sell them dirt cheap!" Or "We guarantee to give you cash for your clunker – no matter how ugly it looks!"

Advertising defects is one thing. But what about when you are dealing face-to-face with a client?

If you work in sales such as automobile, insurance, or real estate , presenting an objection before it surfaces can be dicey. You can easily lose a deal by pointing out a defect, because most buyers are afraid of making a wrong decision.

But it can help your buyer focus on what is most important. After all, in real estate, many purchasers start out wanting a mansion but will settle for much less – especially here in Los Angeles!

So presenting an objectionable item may help to speed up the decision-making process. Advancing an objection helps them sort out in their minds what is most important to them.

I suggest that salespeople use the "Feel, felt, found" technique when dealing with any objection. The reason "feel, felt found" works well is because most sales are made by emotions and then backed up by reason and logic. Feelings are emotions, aren't they?

Here is how this technique works: the words "feel, felt, found" are always used in this exact order with these exact phrases: "I understand how you feel." "Many people have felt this way," "but what we have found is this... blah, blah, blah." Now state your most compelling solution at the very end.

Let's suppose you are an Internet marketer selling a website to a doctor.

The doctor says, "All of this website stuff is well and good, but people come to me based on word of mouth advertising and referrals. I don't need a new website."

Bob: "I get it. You feel there is no need for an expensive new website, is that right?

Doctor: "Exactly."

Bob: "I understand how you feel Dr. Proctor, and many people have felt the same way as you. Money is tight these days. However, what we have found is that more and more customers are now checking out video testimonials posted on YouTube and Facebook. A newer website would allow us to post those videos quickly and easily, but your old website doesn't have that flexibility."

Note: Will this technique work every time? No. But what are we trying to increase? **Your sales percentages**. Try using "feel, felt, found" and see how it works for you.

Selling Outside the Square Perspective 4

Here is another observation of mine: I have noticed that a gentle touch helps when using the feel, felt, found technique.

A light touch on the person's arm, elbow or shoulder seems to make people more aware. I usually do this when saying "many people have felt this way." I touch their arm to let them know that it's okay. They're not crazy. Other humans feel the same way.

For example, if I was hosting a Tupperware party and thought a customer seemed interested in a product, I would lightly touch her arm or shoulder, and then point the beauty or benefits of the product. Why?

Researchers have revealed that a brief touch can have an amazing effect. In a research experiment performed by Nicolas Gueguen, an experimenter approached pedestrians and asked if they could spare a dime.

The first experiment was conducted without touching the upper arm. Then a touch was added. Gueguen discovered that just a brief touch on the upper arm **increased the likelihood of getting the money by 20 percent.** So if you are a waiter, waitress, or multi-level marketer keep this idea in mind!

Richard Wiseman's excellent book, *59 Seconds* talks about how social scientists believe that a friendly touch releases the feel good hormone oxytocin and blocks cortisol, the stress hormone.

A touch and/or a brief hug actually make your client like you because you are forcing the release of those chemicals.

So if you are involved in sales, try using the briefest of touches on the upper arm of your client, but take care on how you do this – especially if you are a guy dealing with a woman.

Touching sends off a strong social signal that you find the other person attractive, therefore you don't want an innocent touch to turn into a claim of groping.

And if you discover that your Millennial client does not warm to the touch, don't do it. Sexual harassment is a touchy subject and you don't want to be viewed as a creep.

**"Me, creepy?
No way!"**

Trigger #5: Use Curiosity to Sell

Have you ever heard the saying that goes, "Curiosity Killed the Cat?" How does it work in sales? One way that advertisers use curiosity is to make items wet and shining.

Car photographers do this because researchers have found that most people are naturally drawn to and curious about shiny objects. Many magazine ads will feature sleek cars, diamond rings, and glistening metal knowing that we will seek them out. One scientific study found that pedestrians who were walking down a street would pause and slow down MORE for a gleaming storefront window than a dull one. Why? The theory is that being drawn to glistening objects is evolutionary in nature because in one experiment, when infants saw a shiny plate they tried to lick it.

Some scientists believe that at one time the ability to see shiny objects enabled our ancestors to find clear drinking water. Interesting, isn't it?

Beyond using immaculate, glossy objects to arouse curiosity though, many advertisers are fond of keeping eyes glued to sales copy by describing what something means to YOU in mysterious, vague terms. Doing so forces people to continue to read on to find out what the benefit will be for them. After all, most people – especially those belonging to the Millennial crowd **are more interested in themselves** than in others.

If I was to take a photograph of you along with thirteen other people, and then later showed you the picture, who would you look for **FIRST** in the picture?

Would you look for yourself first?

Yep! We humans are curious creatures, aren't we?

Yes, we are a little vain, too. But if you are surrounded by other people when someone snaps a photograph, you might be wondering: How does my hair look? Did I blink? Did I leave the barn door accidentally open?

Strip-tease artists know how important curiosity is to their customers.

They take off a little here and something there to hold your interest.

Advertisers know that you think about yourself too and for this reason, many will use the word "you." Here is an example of an ad that I found in the National Enquirer that uses curiosity along with the word "you" or "your."

This secret is incredibly simple. Anyone can use it. You can get started with practically no money at all, and people will be literally eating out of your hand. Best of all, your friends will be shedding pounds while eating their favorite desert! After all, who can't resist digging into a rich, moist piece of chocolate cake! Yes, your friends will say that you're making dieting a piece of cake!

Selling Outside of the Square Perspective 5

How can I best use curiosity to become more successful in sales?

A good first start might be to be curious about **your** business.

Ask yourself this question, "What is the most profitable segment of my business?"

Then ask, "How can I do more of that?" Knowing what IS profitable and what IS NOT may give you greater motivation to focus on doing what is profitable.

In the reality TV show, *Hell's Kitchen*, Chef Gordon Ramsay demonstrated to a bar owner that he would make more money offering four higher-priced, delicious items on the menu than 24 cheaper ones. Chef Ramsey also put a GenMe-looking bartender in charge as chef. He showed the young man how to cook the four items and then sales blasted off. The bar once again became profitable. Can you improve sales by eliminating unprofitable items? Or can you change the person in charge of a certain action to help become more profitable?

If you are a Millennial salesperson, knowing that "curiosity killed the cat" might give you a clue about yourself. Consider saving your own curiosity as a reward.

Your thinking might go something like this: because I know that I am a curious human, just for today I am going to fight the temptation to browse Facebook, Twitter or Google myself. I will update my Facebook status after I make my 150 sales calls. So just for today, I am going to follow a strict routine.

I am going to make a step-by-step plan and stick to it for 30 solid days.

I am going to tell other people about my goals. (This will make them curious to see whether I can keep them and will motivate me as well.) Try it!

Trigger #6: Commitment and Consistency

Would you like to be known as a wishy-washy person who changes his/her mind anytime the wind blows a certain way? Or would you rather be known as a person of commitment and consistency? Most people like to be thought of as being consistent. After all, inconsistent people are looked upon as being fickle, uncertain or scatterbrained.

We view a consistent person as being rational, assured, trustworthy, and sound. For this reason, most people are reluctant to be thought of as inconsistent.

In sales, we want people to view us as being consistent but also we want our buyers to stick up to their side of the contract too. That's why we put our agreements in writing. We write down goals too, because once we make public our stand on an issue the more likely we will act consistent with it.

According to master sales trainer Tom Hopkins, the idea in sales is to lead the prospect to a decision by asking easy-to-answer questions. Or as the comedian Bill Murray would say in the movie, *"What About Bob"* take baby steps. "Baby steps, baby steps!"

If you are a salesperson, each easy-to-answer question that you ask is like a baby-step. When the prospect gives you a "yes" answer, consider it a commitment that allows you to ask another question that leads to another baby step, and on and on.

Therefore, if I can get you to take a small stand or go on record by saying "yes," I will have set the stage for another consistent step based on that earlier commitment. Once a stand is taken, there is a natural tendency to behave in ways that are consistent with the stand. Let's say, for example, that I want you to purchase a peach pie for my school, I might ask something easy to answer:

"Do you think high school sports are important?" "Yes, I do."

"Do you like to eat pies?" Yes.

"Do you like peach pies?" Yes.

"Because our basketball team is trying to raise money for new uniforms, would you consider buying a peach pie that we are selling for our school?" Um, Maybe.

But what if I were to ask, "Would you like to buy a peach pie for our school today?" What might you say? "No." "Why not?" "Because I don't like peaches. Or "I don't like pies."

A scientific experiment conducted by Freedman and Fraser concerning a large, poorly lettered sign may help to better explain this point. Researchers went door-to-door in a neighborhood lugging a large, ugly sign that read, "Drive Carefully." When homeowners were first approached about having the sign planted in their front yard, 83% declined the privilege.

In a second neighborhood that was similar to the first however, 76% of the homeowners agreed to post the same ugly sign in their front yards. What caused the homeowners in the second neighborhood to act differently?

Approximately two weeks earlier, the second group of homeowners had been asked by a female volunteer to display a 3-inch sign in their front yard.

This sign read "Be a safe driver." Most homeowners thought nothing of it, but when the same requester came back asking the homeowners to really show their civic duty and support their community by displaying the big, ugly sign, most felt duty-bound to oblige her. Researchers claim that **any small commitment** that you can get a prospective customer to agree to will help with getting a bigger commitment along that path.

Selling Outside the Square Perspective 6

A good small commitment to ask from a Millennial might be **an email address.** Most folks don't mind giving out their email address, do they?

I have mentioned the service where a person sends a text message to a number posted on a sign.

The beauty of using this service is not only does the Millennial client receive the requested information instantly, but the salesperson will also receive a copy of the customer's cell phone number. So if you are a salesperson, you could send them a text at a later time if you wish.

What about getting ALL the email addresses from an entire tract of homes?

If you wanted to get all the email addresses from an entire neighborhood, hold a vacation contest or a contest to win a coupon for $50 worth of groceries. Be sure to mention that the winner will be notified via email, so it better be a good email address!

In exchange for getting an email address, **you could also offer a coupon for YOUR product or service.** This coupon can be emailed to customers with a suggestion to send a copy to their friends or relatives before the expiration date. In fact, many restaurants leave a large tip jar near the exit door – and even salt the jar with a few business cards so that customers get the idea of leaving a business card. After all, most business cards nowadays will have the person's email address on them, won't they?

Besides creating a small commitment from a customer, why is collecting email addresses a good idea for a restaurant or other business? Communication via email helps to develop rapport with many GenMe customers. Many of them religiously check email messages on their iPhones. If you contact people via email from 8 a.m. to 5 p.m. you stand a chance of them opening it and responding to your message.

So if you owned a restaurant and it's Monday morning and you figure that six tables might be empty tonight, could an email blast help your sales?

Advertise a "free Monday dessert" or "drink special Monday?" Include a "call to action" such as "Stop by now" "Call me now" "Buy now." Could consistently sending emails eventually help draw in customers? It certainly might.

There are a number of free emailing companies that allow a person to stay in contact with people on their email lists. The one I use is called www.mailchimp.com. It's free and as good a place to start as AWeber or Constant Contact or some of the other paid services. You can also export your email list if you wish to upgrade to a paid service.

And if you would like to find out the next trigger, let's move on!

Trigger #7: The Scarcity Principle

Will Rogers once said, "Buy real estate because they ain't making any more of it." This quote helps to describe the principle of scarcity. This principle says that when the average person realizes that something is in short supply or might be soon, he will want it even more. Baseball cards, bicycles, art, weird, odd and just plain ugly objects often become collectible and more valuable after time. Why?

Simply because other people have thrown them away and now they have become rare.

How to use the scarcity principle in sales is simple: Make up false deadlines, offer limited opportunities or present limited production numbers such as "there are only a limited number of these items available."

"After Monday the price will go up because our costs have risen!"

Here is another example. I might use scarcity with this book. I could tell you: "This book is in short supply. There are only three left, and a man from the bookstore across town just purchased the last three. However, there might be one or two in the back room. If I find one, I'm not sure what condition it will be in, I think this might be the edition with the mistake in it, but if I autograph it, will you take it?" You might think to yourself: *Wow, a flawed object, with an autograph by the author. That sounds rare! I want it even more!*

Selling Outside the Square Perspective 7

Use the scarcity principle with additional bonuses to motivate a Millennial buyer: "If you order by March 1st, we guarantee that you will receive these three valuable bonuses! But hurry, they're going fast!"

The cookie experiment shows how the shortage of an object can affect a GenMe person's perception of its quality.

Here's what I mean. An experiment was done where subjects were asked to pick the taste of cookies from two cookie jars.

Students were told that both containers started out with 85 cookies that were freshly baked earlier that morning.

The time now is 3:00 p.m. and subjects are asked to rate the taste of the two cookies.

 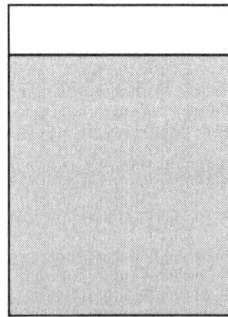

Cookie "A"   Cookie "B"

Both cookie jars started with the same number of cookies. Which cookie do you think tastes better? Cookie A with 2 cookies, or Cookie B with 79 left in the jar?

Which cookie would YOU guess tasted better to the subjects?

If you said cookies from Cookie Jar A, give yourself a pat on the back!

People assumed that because more of them were taken from the jar, those cookies must have tasted better. But that's not all. Scarcity can also imply that something might cost more too, can't it?

If I told you that the cookies from Cookie Jar A **cost more** than the ones from Cookie B, would you believe me?

The reality is that **both cookie jars had the same cookies made on the same day at the same time**!

So if you are looking to sell products to Me Generation buyers consider offering items that might have a scarcity factor. Look for items that might appeal to individualistic tastes and/or things that help display a feeling of confidence or coolness. Some examples include: sunglasses, clothing, tennis shoes, new cell phones, video games and beauty or anti-aging products. Consider personalizing products to make them more unique. Add something distinctive to a hum-drum product and it may boost your sales.

The Scarcity Principle in Reverse

If you are a Millennial salesperson, realize that the scarcity principle works in reverse too. This means that your company may **NOT** see you as being extremely rare or "one of a kind".

Me Generation salespeople may secretly think "NOBODY can replace ME," but the reality may be far different. So be committed to your job. Get serious. Show up early or at least on time. Don't act like you're entitled to special privileges too. When you signed an employment agreement, you signed a contract for employment. Your company expects you to honor that commitment and NOT be cavalier about it.

So **AVOID** saying things like:

"That's not my job"

"What's the big deal?"

"I can't work with Joe"

"My bad"

"Can you do this for me?"

Even the phrase **"What would you do without me?"** can backfire big-time. A manager might think, "What would I do without you sounds like you are testing me. Hmm. I bet the new person Omar can handle things better than she does. Plus we'd actually save some money by getting rid of her salary." **Lose the idea that you deserve special treatment.** Your hard work, humility and willingness to cooperate with others WILL help you win respect. But being a Prima Donna just poisons it.

Tell-tale Signs of a Prima Donna

I am 100% Diva

Glamour

Style

100% bitch

i'm kinda difficult

It's not my fault

100% Girl

Gurlz Day is Every Day

All I want is the world

Buy me a big diamond ring

Trigger # 8: Social Proof

Have you ever heard one of your parents utter these pearls of wisdom: **"Well, if so and so jumped off a cliff, would you follow him?"** This in a nutshell is social proof - the idea that someone else's behavior is more correct than your own, simply because someone else is doing it. Here's a personal example.

A friend of mine gave me tickets for *American Idol* and I was sitting in the audience enjoying the show. I was surrounded on all sides by relatives and ardent fans of one particular singer. In fact, he is a man so nice, they named him twice. His mother was sitting in front of me. So when his performance was over, and all these people rose to their feet and started applauding wildly, guess what I did? Yep. I was on my feet, cheering too.

Ever wonder what caused the mortgage meltdown? I think it's time to stop blaming President George W. Bush and the U.S. Congress and realize that **social proof** pure and simple might have had something to do with the mortgage meltdown.

People run banks and a CEO responds the same way to social proof as anyone else.

Therefore, if I'm the CEO of a bank and a lot of other banks are using **a 585 FICO** score as the minimum criteria to make a risky loan, I'm thinking that maybe our bank should be doing the same thing.

After all, the other banks may know something that we don't.

Like airplanes locked onto automatic pilot, their controllers never looking out the window to see the mountain looming ahead, the banks continued to make risky loan after risky loan until they crashed.

Sad, but true.

Selling Outside of the Square Perspective 8

Most Millennials think of themselves as individuals, yet actually they are just as susceptible to moving in predictable patterns as anybody else. Basic human nature tells us that if you don't know which way to go, follow someone else's cue. Not sure of what to eat at a restaurant? Look around and see what others are enjoying. It's like the funny scene from the movie *When Harry Met Sally*, "I'll have what she's having."

We are such sheep that researchers have found that most Americans like to walk counter-clockwise when they grocery shop. Who do you think visits the grocery store more often, men or women? So what does a grocery store like Vons do? Vons will put fresh-smelling products and bright colors- immediately to the right of the entrance, so that when a woman enters, her senses are instantly assaulted with the scent of fresh flowers and the sight of lively colors. She probably sees the shiny, gleaming chrome in the produce section too.

How do we use social proof to help improve sales?

A story from **www.cracked.com** concerning Alka Seltzer mentions how this company used social proof to sell more of their product.

Sales of Alka Seltzer were doing okay, but management wanted to boost production so they created a television spot that showed a hand opening an Alka Seltzer package and dropping two tablets into a large glass of water.

Then the jingle would start, "Plop, plop, fizz, fizz" – okay, wait. Do you know the rest of the words? This is a GenMe age test because many of them don't know the rest of the jingle.

(The correct answer is "Oh what a relief it is.)

The brilliant social proof sales idea was to show that TWO Alka Seltzer tablets were needed to cure a hangover – or whatever the ailment was. The truth is that only ONE tablet was necessary. But taking two tablets wouldn't kill anyone, plus it would improve sales tremendously – especially if people THOUGHT they had to take two pills for the product to work.

On that same note, Costco and other box stores increase product sales by marketing items in bulk. Purchasing 12 cans of Campbell's Chunky soup costs almost as much as buying six, yet inevitably, a person doesn't use all 12 and ends up noticing the expiration date and ~~donating~~ throwing out spoiled goods. Can you do this with your product? (That is, sell more products in bulk?)

Another example of a product that benefited from using social proof involves Johnny Walker scotch. Sales of this scotch were gradually going downhill so around the holiday season, the company decided to substantially increase the price and portray the scotch as one of the finest tasting whiskeys in the world (though that part was debatable.)

The whiskey came wrapped in a nicely decorated holiday gift box – and made a splendid gift for that classy executive or beautiful woman someone wanted to impress.

Question: Would the average Joe know the difference between a good tasting scotch and a bad one? Nope. It's 86 proof; doesn't that mean it's a good scotch? The taste of scotch whiskey is subjective; and in this case, marketers showed celebrities touting the stuff in *Playboy Magazine*. Despite the fact that the whiskey carried a hefty price tag, social proof made people draw a "wow" assumption when they received a bottle of Johnny Walker scotch. It must be of good quality because it was featured in Playboy, celebrities liked it, and the company charged big bucks for the stuff. It "wowed" people and as expected, sales of the whiskey rocketed upwards.

Moving along, how can you "wow" a cynical Millennial customer with social proof?

The way to a Millennial customer's heart is to take a creative, visual approach. Try to express the feeling that a buyer will encounter when using your product or service and create a simple 30 second commercial or video testimonial on www.animoto.com. Explain who you are, what you do and what to expect.

In Charles Duhigg's best-selling book, *The Power Of Habit: Why We Do What We Do In Life And In Business* he mentions how the marketers at Proctor & Gamble studied videos of people making their beds. Why? Because the P&G marketers were desperate to figure out how to sell a product that was on track to be one of the biggest flops in company history.

The P&G product was supposedly strong enough to remove skunk odor from a bedroom but the marketers couldn't figure out how to sell it to their target market - Millennial housewives.

Suddenly, one of the marketers made an astute observation. He noticed a pattern. After some younger housewives had completed their bed-making chore these women would spray the air and bedspread with the new Proctor & Gamble product and give a sigh of relief. These women appeared to be rewarding themselves on a job well done by liberally spraying the product around the bed.

The P&G marketers believed that by using this example as social proof and a bit of TV advertising along with a name-change, the P&G product, now called **Febreze** could be a big success. Sure enough, Febreze went on to earn a billion dollars that year.

Again, if you are marketing to a Millennial buyer, try to create visual social proof of **the feeling** that someone might associate with your product. Make it eye candy. People who are unsure about which product, person or service to choose, may just decide on you or your firm because of the simple fact that someone else "liked" you or your video on Facebook or shared it on YouTube!

Trigger # 9: Reciprocation

Reciprocation means that most people will often give back to you when you give back to them. After all, every religious book says "give out first, then receive." And in sales, a large body of research shows that doing a favor for someone often results in getting back more in return.

A research experiment by Dennis Regan done in the 1970s showed that when a research subject was given a soda, and later asked to donate 0.25 to purchase a raffle ticket, the research subject was not only more apt to return the favor, but would often buy **more than double** the amount of tickets by subjects not offered the free soda.

Doing a favor is a powerful motivator especially when you do something from the heart, and not the head. Ask for the return favor quickly, though, because people nowadays get too busy to return anything, especially favors.

Usually people will offer a free sample to get the reciprocity wheel rolling. You often see this tactic used on the Internet. To download a free report – just leave your email address.

Later, after getting the info you may also receive 7 more emails plus a guilt trip for not purchasing an expensive training course!

How about box supermarkets like Price Club and Costco? There you'll see food stations set up for customers to taste and sample new products.

After sampling the item, many folks will reciprocate by purchasing it. Interestingly, at these box-stores, the price point for a single item is slightly lower and you feel like you are getting a better deal because you receive a larger amount of the product.

So you might think to yourself, "OMG, what a score. I got such a great bargain!" And not, "Buying five pounds of shellfish might not be a good idea because I am single woman without any children and have no need for so much shrimp." So it's not uncommon for these stores to use this technique and thereby multiply sales.

Thinking Outside the Square Perspective 9

One thing that can't be quantified with reciprocity is that when you do something with love, and not for gain, your results can quadruple. My firm belief is that the real estate market can go to hell in a hand basket, **but there will always be people buying homes.**

Why? Because a home is more than a house. It's where memories are made and people are cherished.

A home equals love. No matter what people think they are purchasing, they are buying love. At least that's what I sell my clients.

When the mortgage meltdown occurred, my wife and I helped homeowners modify their loans. The idea wasn't to list their homes it was to help people **stay** in their homes.

Was everyone able to successfully modify their home loan? No. Did some owners have to sell their homes? Yes. Did we list those homes? Yes.

Ironically, we listed several homes even though we failed at getting help for the owners. So the reciprocity rule basically states, "If you scratch my back, I will scratch yours, or I will do my best to do so."

This is the beauty of reciprocity- the favor returned does NOT have to be the same exact thing given. If I borrow seven hundred dollars from you today and I am a drug rehab specialist, but I don't have the funds to repay you tomorrow, I might pay you back by helping your loved one get off drugs. This might be worth MORE to you than the actual money amount. So think along those lines too, especially when it comes to the Millennial people you will encounter.

Knowing that Millennials like individuality, is there a way to personalize the item for reciprocity? A friend of mine is a Network Marketer. She primarily promotes diet products but offers her Internet marketing services in exchange for allowing her products to be displayed at various brick and mortar businesses around town. For example, she will:

- Write an article
- Retweet or forward an article to her 10,000 Twitter followers
- Announce job openings on her newsletter
- Share links
- Solicit feedback on projects
- Offer discounts or coupons to prospective clients
- Encourage testimonials

In other words, she knows that most local businesses don't like to promote themselves online or via social media because it makes them look cheesy. So she promotes these services and in exchange they promote her NM products in their brick and mortar stores. To people online it appears the promotion is coming from someone else, and not the business. It's a win-win.

Can you think of a way to help out a business owner? Is there something he or she might NOT like to do themselves that you could do for them? Something that's as easy as a piece of cake. Perhaps there has been a Federal emergency declared because of a hurricane. Homeowners may need help getting a forbearance agreement from their lender. Perhaps you could do the paperwork?

Be on the lookout for items in the news. Perhaps an oil spill has stopped drilling in the Gulf of Mexico and you are an expert in the petroleum clean-up field. Maybe you can offer an expert endorsement of a product that could make oil clean-up safer. In return, that company will sponsor your church's efforts to stamp out hunger in Africa.

Speaking of experts, this brings me to our next trigger: authority.

Trigger # 10: Authority

There was once a television commercial where a celebrity actor dressed like a doctor proclaimed, "I'm not a doctor, but I play one on TV."

"Trust me, I'm NOT a doctor"

Having read that sentence, would you take health advice from this person? No. You would be crazy to, right? But sales of the product, Sanka instant coffee actually DOUBLED when this commercial first aired.

Advertisers were not mystified because they knew the secret of using an authority figure in a commercial. If you can get an expert or a celebrity's endorsement, the product has a better chance of selling. Right? Well, perhaps half-right on this trigger.

Celebrity endorsements do seem to carry more weight with Millennial customers than experts do. Perhaps it is because the message that most Millennials have heard all their life is a materialistic one: that we should have it all, do it all, and be it all.

Then we will be happy, and if we're not, there must be something seriously wrong with us!

Celebrities best represent this Millennial message because advertising often portrays them as being happy, beautiful and worry free. Therefore if Jennifer Lopez looks stylish wearing that makeup and Macy's outfit, then I will look fashionable and happy wearing it too. But when an expert on fashion makes a comment on the way the Me Generation person looks, many GenMe'ers will disagree:

"What makes him or her a fashion "expert?" they will say.

"What do they know, anyway?"

(Isn't that what many losing contestants utter after failing a blind audition on *American Idol*?)

Thinking Outside the Square Perspective10

The biggest thing to remember with Millennial customers is that they are very wary of "so-called experts" and staunchly believe that their own needs are paramount.

The world revolves around them, remember?

Teachers often complain about this.

They say that GenMe students are too contrarian because there are times when GenMe takes the questioning of authority a little too far. Here is an excerpt from the book *Generation Me*:

"Education professor Maureen Stout tells the story of a young man in her class who did not turn in his research paper. 'After a lot of excuses and arguments he finally came out with it.' Stout writes. 'He believed he was entitled to do as he pleased and refused to recognize my authority, as the instructor, to determine what the assignments in the class should be. It was as simple as that.'"

The Me Generation's attitude seems to be, "Even though you may be older than me and have more life experiences, what makes you think that you know more than me? Or are better than me?'"

A GenMe person can't be that cynical, can they?

Yes they can.

By the way, even though you may not have been born during the years of the Millennials, and YOU are respectful to others, guess what? You are now a part of the Me Generation's culture because this view has become the prevailing attitude and feeling in America today.

You might be thinking, that's not fair, I am not like that – yet look around you and you'll see that many of the Millennial notions have crept into your life as silently as crabgrass takes over a bluegrass lawn.

The accepted wisdom may be there already without you even realizing it. The Me Generation way of thinking has become the accepted way for most people in America. Again, I am not being judgmental. I'm just trying to make you more aware.

Case in point: Is it okay for a 65 year old woman to get a facelift? Yes. Is it okay for a 43 year old woman to get a tummy-tuck? I guess so. Is it okey-dokey for a 26 year old woman to get breast augmentation surgery? What would most people say? **Sure. Why not? If it makes her feel better, fine, let her go ahead and do it. Right?**

But see, that's the prevailing attitude of Generation Me. Twenty years ago most people would have instantly said the correct answer is: "No. She is only 26. It is more important for her to save money for a down payment on a house or to pay off her credit cards."

These days the answer is "Yes, because a 26 year old woman has the right to spend her money on any surgery if it will make her feel better. It's her money."

Say I visit a Millennial customer's home. If I tell Mr. GenMe seller that his home should be priced at $300,000 based on the facts of what has sold and my experience, guess what often happens? Mr. Millennial Seller will probably laugh and tell me to pound sand. Why? Because who really wants to be the big shot, the diva, the info king or the authority figure? That's right, Mr. Millennial Seller.

He will usually update me on every sale in the neighborhood too because he has checked them out on Zillow.com. So my advice to sales people involved in belly-to-belly selling is to act more like Detective Columbo: be humble, politely persistent, yet deadly specific.

You remember Columbo, don't you? In the first few minutes of this TV detective mystery, a smart and wealthy killer commits a murder and then LAPD detective Columbo has to figure out how he or she did it. (You can find the entire series of Columbo available on NetFlix.)

The killers are much smarter than Colombo, aren't they? He's just a bumbling idiot who drives an old car.

Yet Columbo manages to crack cases by asking questions, listening politely and taking lots of notes. He usually nails the killer on something specific too. So don't be afraid to be doggedly persistent and put your palm to your forehead and ask a pointed question: "Just one more thing, sir. The house that sold for $325,000, that was the home with the tan imported bathroom tile, wasn't it?" Ouch, that didn't show up on Zillow.com. This is probably one of your best ways to deal with some Millennial customers. Be politely persistent. Yet deadly specific.

After all, if a Millennial customer has had a bad experience, what will they do? He or she will not only scream bloody murder but they will also post a nasty review on Yelp, Facebook, and Twitter too!

They will tell the entire world about you and their dreadful incident.

Here's an example of a woman who liked the food at a restaurant but didn't get her soda refilled fast enough.

Why? Because the person working behind the counter was (gasp) helping another customer!

Here is her actual review from Yelp.com:

I'm all for supporting local businesses. In fact, I'm always the one to suggest it when I go out with friends or family, that's why I suggested we eat at XYZ Restaurant. The food there; I have to say is really good. Portions are decent, but those people at the counter should be better trained. I go back to ask for a refill on my soda and the guy behind the counter completely ignores me while taking someone else's order RIGHT IN FRONT OF ME!!! (He saw me!!!) WTF!!!!!!!!!!!!!!!!!!!!!!!! @^#%$&$(&!^$^$*. Not cool! I like your food, but the bad attitude from you guys is not worth my time, money or sanity!

OMG! I think somebody should switch to de-caffeinated ~~Sanka~~. The Internet is full of hateful reviews and there is a whole category of computer specialists who do nothing but "reputation management." They command as much as $800 a month to repair a business's damaged reputation as a result of a bad review.

My point is this: if you can get testimonials from doctors, celebrities and experts in your field, do so. On the positive side, a review from a satisfied GenMe customer with a smart-phone and 5 minutes of time can be worth its weight in gold. Some GenMe'ers will even gladly create a YouTube or Facebook video post, if you are persistent and ask them politely.

Also if you own a business consider varying delivery systems for your products.

A realtor or insurance agent, for example, might have downloadable forms that a GenMe customer might be able to review in advance as well as go over in person.

If you are a restaurant owner, perhaps you should install a self-service soda dispenser. That way, a customer doesn't have to bother the counter-person to get a refill.

Some sushi places have conveyor belts that offer plates of sushi with prices varying depending upon the color of the plate. So customers get instant gratification - they don't have to waste valuable time waiting for the sushi chef to prepare the raw fish.

A better example of varying delivery systems might be a real estate lender who can deliver papers instantly via email, or via an app or an online portal. Most Millennial buyers would appreciate that approach; however, the lender might also consider delivering documents the "old school" way too like using Fed Ex or overnight mail. Don't just assume that everyone wants to print out 75 pages on their home computer.

A few years ago when my escrow officer told me that she needed to wire the closing funds to the title company, I asked her a dumb question. I asked if she could wire my commission check to my bank. She said, "Yes" and I've been doing it ever since. It helps save trees and avoids an extra trip to the bank too!

Look for ways to vary delivery systems to your clients and your customer service ratings may be rewarded! For information about the next trigger, let's move on!

Trigger #11: Just Like Me!

People like to do business with people they like. That's a no-brainer. After all, with all things considered, wouldn't you rather give a person you trust your business than a stranger? But interestingly, people also prefer to do business with folks they consider to be physically attractive yet familiar with too. Therefore, the more the salesperson is like the customer; the more the customer will like the salesperson!

Similarly, when somebody "likes" what you have posted on Facebook, you will often "like" something they post.

Physical attractiveness plus familiarity also makes it easier for a voter to associate with a candidate because whomever you vote for represents you. When he wins, you win. In politics today, it also helps to have a familiar name like Bush, Reagan or Clinton – because most people are readily familiar with those names. They are like "brand names" that are already associated with politics

It also helps to be good looking. People like to root for attractive people without really knowing why.

Studies have shown that favorable traits such as honesty, kindness and intelligence are subconsciously assigned to good-looking people.

Subconsciously, your brain says: a handsome person equals a product that I want because I want to be like that attractive person.

But people also like to do business with people who like them.

Question: how can you tell that somebody likes you or that you like them? Here's a hint: **Compliment them**. A comedian once joked, "My wife tricked me into marrying her. She told me that she liked me."

Linda is a mom with three children who sells Avon products door-to-door. When she rings a doorbell, she told me that she greets every new face with a smile and a compliment such as, "Oh I just love the flowers in your planter."

We don't know if Linda is attractive, but did you notice what she did? She complimented the homeowner and smiled. Often all it takes to show someone that you like them is to throw out an admiring comment- and smile.

Gee, aren't you a smart reader. (Grin)

If the woman at the door has children, the next thing Linda can do is talk about her children. Linda likes flowers, so does the homeowner. They are like each other.

Does it help that Linda is attractive? Of course. But the fact that Linda smiles, offers a kind word, and has things in common with the homeowner pushes the likeability factor even more. And when people like you and trust you, they will buy from you.

Celebrities are often not only good-looking people, but likeable too, so it's no wonder why advertisers want them associated with their products. If a winner is associated with a product, then maybe if I use that product, I will be seen as a winner too.

But what if it's difficult to associate liking with a particular product?

During the 2012 Summer Olympics, sponsored by McDonald's, viewers were asked to make a somewhat unusual association.

Olympic athletes are often known for their strict diets yet were being sponsored by a fast- food company accused of causing obesity in America for its cholesterol-choked cheeseburgers, fries and shakes.

But instead of inviting complaints about their TV ads, most people loved one commercial in particular. Called "Rivals," this commercial cleverly used McDonald's food as a reward for games involving friendly competition between two people.

The ad starts with a girl who challenges her friend in a running race to a distant tree, the winner will get a McDonald's Happy Meal as the reward. The ad moves to showcase other people from around the world engaged in friendly games of competition: one-on-one basketball, swimming to the other side of the pool, and playing soccer. None of them are Olympic athletes, but they are involved in friendly competitions with the prize being McDonald's food.

One girl has a Spanish accent, one boy is Japanese and the soccer players are from other countries, just like the Olympics features athletes from other countries.

Then the silhouette of a likeable U.S. Olympic athlete, basketball star LeBron James appears beside another U.S Olympic basketball player. The player to the side of LeBron, looks up longingly at the American flag.

"For the gold medal," he says.

"And a Big Mac," LeBron replies.

The message is that not only will friendly rivals all over the world - just like you and me work extra hard to win a McDonald's hamburger, but so will an engaging Olympic celebrity like LeBron James. He is just like us and we are like him. If he likes McDonald's then we like McDonald's too!

Thinking Outside the Square Perspective 11

Salespeople who market Avon, Tupperware, Amway or other Network Marketing products often use likeability.

Millennials are perfect for it too. Why? Because most Generation Me folks are *starved* to hear a bit of flattery. Someone may have "liked" a Facebook comment but that's almost like eating fast-food. There's little nutritional content in a Facebook "like." So give an honest to goodness, home-cooked personal accolade like "Gee, you look pretty tonight" or "You have such a beautiful smile." Most Millennials are hungry for praise and starving for appreciation. Feed them a compliment and give them a smile whenever you can.

Up-selling is a part of likeability. What is up-selling? Up-selling is just bundling another product with an order to make a bigger sale.

For example, you have ordered a hamburger so what's the harm in asking, "Would you like some fries with that?" Can you add another item to up-sell your customers?

Likeability can extend to products that you sell online too. For example, you don't have to attend meetings, have Tupperware parties or knock on doors to sell things. All it takes nowadays to make extra money is to send out emails to your friends and family members with a review of a product you like.

Let's suppose you enjoyed reading this book. You could send a copy to a friend and hope they will return it one day in the not-too-distant future.

Or you could send your friend to a website like http://www.sellingoutsidethesquare.com where they could purchase a copy of the book themselves.

When your pal buys the book, YOU would make some money and not have to worry about never seeing your book again!

One Amazon affiliate made over $600,000 promoting books online.

To become an Amazon affiliate or associate, first join and fill out an easy application at https://affiliate-program.amazon.com/. Then find a book like this to sell. Secure the Amazon Associate coded link for the product and save it as a text file. Then make a YouTube video about it and include the link on the very first line. Then when you talk about the book in the video, tell people to hit the link below and point downward. It works! Then send the YouTube video review to your friends. You can also include the link when you run a Google or Facebook ad campaign. You can also market the product to a list or group that you believe may benefit from the book.

Interestingly, research studies show that people are even willing to pay a little more to deal with a salesperson they like.

A recent poll by the Carlisle & Gallegher Consulting Group claimed that one third of all potential borrowers would pay a higher rate if the mortgage process was smoother and they had one point of contact to help guide them through the lending process.

Most salespeople will look for ways to improve their likeability by establishing rapport with a customer.

If a car salesperson sees a tennis racquet in the back seat of a prospect's car, the salesperson might make a remark about it or about tennis – even though the salesperson may not like the sport.

"I noticed your tennis racquet, is that for air-guitar or do you really play?" the salesperson might ask. "I play every day at the YMCA," answers the prospect.

"The YMCA by Kohl's?" "Yes, that's the one." "My wife loves to shop at Kohl's." "Really? So does my wife."

You are like me and therefore I like you.

In fact, some salespeople will purposely "mirror and match" to imitate a prospect's posture, hand gestures and head movements. Why? To be more like the prospect. Science shows that even these tiny details help to increase the likelihood of making a sale. We like people who are like us. The three most popular words in the English language are: you, money and save. And the three most popular combinations of words, by David Peoples in his book, *Presentations Plus* are: Thank you, would you please? And what do you think?

Finally, like the McDonald's commercial starring LeBron James, is there a way that you can create a connection with your product and a Hawaiian vacation?

After all, most people would love to travel to Hawaii – especially during the winter months. Can you create a sales campaign to win a trip to Hawaii?

To enter, applicants must supply a good working email address.

Not only will your product or service receive some likeability juice from the Hawaiian vacation but you can continue to market these clients throughout the year with other products and services.

Yes, there will be freebie seekers who will never buy anything, but they may also tell two or three of their friends who *will* buy.

Trigger #12: Tell the Truth!

Your mother probably told you to always tell the truth, and though you might not think so, doing so can help you make more sales! Here is why: the modern world moves at a frantic pace and to survive, we depend upon short cuts.

An honest person, who tells us the truth no matter how ugly it is, actually saves us time. For example, if a product is popular, it means that many people are purchasing it. But does it also mean the product is good?

No, not necessarily because according to social proof, I might buy it, because my friends are purchasing it. It's "monkey see, monkey do." When a funny movie called *The Hangover* came out, I saw it first and loved it, so I persuaded two of my high school pals who hadn't seen the movie to join me. They loved it too!

When the sequel, *Hangover 2* came out, one of my buddies rushed to see it first.

When I asked him what he thought of the movie, he was honest.

"Just rent it," he muttered and I didn't question him.

Even though I heard positive opinions from other people, I trusted my friend because he knows my taste in movies. His honesty saved me time and money.

Selling Outside the Square Perspective 12

We have entered an age where any person with a smart device can post a review about a product or service. When it comes to promoting goods and services, honesty is the best policy.

But is that what a Millennial customer really wants to hear?

Well, yes and no.

The truth is that salespeople often resort to making bold claims just to grab your attention. Politicians love to do this too. "I will cut taxes, decrease spending and retire the national debt in one year." Many people love to hear these bold claims because we want to believe that there is a quick and easy fix. Or we want to hold the politician's feet to the fire. Either way, it made us consider the premise.

Bottomline: our lives are moving faster nowadays. Our relationships are shorter. Friends come and go.

In addition, we have an avalanche of information and choices.

We like it when something stands out and grabs our attention. We want to believe in a quick and easy solution to our problems.

In fact, if you could avoid reading this book and instead just take a purple pill to consume the information you would do it, wouldn't you? Sure you would.

That's just the way it is these days, right?

Therefore, if you are going to make a bold claim, be brutally honest. Not long ago I looked on Craigslist for a stove. There were lots of offerings, but then I came across this brutally honest ad that caught my eye.

"We owe $17,300 and need to sell our stove. If you stop by tomorrow and buy it, you will help us avoid bankruptcy and get a great deal on a stove. So please, come "buy" tomorrow!"

This ad appears to be telling the truth about the person's financial situation. Plus he or she seemed motivated, so I went there and purchased the stove.

Most Millennial buyers like everyone else feel overwhelmed with TMI (too much information) and NET (not enough time) syndromes that affect our daily lives. Technology evolves faster than we can keep pace, so people will still rely upon recommendations from friends who will be forthright and direct about your product or service.

After all, why do people go to Craigslist.org? Besides the many ~~kinky~~ personal ads, they go there to buy things. So if you are looking to sell a product, place an ad on Craigslist but be honest.

If you don't get a good response, then add additional product information, more pictures or consider making a video or writing a more detailed ad.

A good idea might be to compare and contrast things with pictures. Ever notice that there are several successful TV shows where old items get restored? People seem to really like these shows. Why not create your own 30 second commercial? We can see:

Before--After | Now--Later | Our Company--The Competitor With our Product --Without our Product

Using pictures helps trigger emotions and strong feelings about products or services. Remember people buy on emotions. So be truthful in your copy, testimonials and pictures or videos about them.

If you are new to business and don't have any testimonials yet, that's okay. Tell about other life experiences you've had. "I have two boys and was involved in the PTA at Meadows Elementary School."

Just be honest.

Conclusion: Where to Go from Here?

This is the last chapter of this book, but before I conclude, I would like you to consider another dumb question: Which happens first, a feeling of happiness then success? Or is it first a feeling of success, then happiness?

You might be surprised to learn that a scientific study was actually done on this topic by Sonja Lyubomirsky at the University of California.

Experiments were performed where people found "lost" money on the street; they read aloud positive affirmations, smelled fresh flowers, watched funny films and did several other things that normally make people feel either happy or successful. But the researchers concluded that first there is a feeling of happiness – then a feeling of success. In other words, success is a result of being happy. Happiness does not come from success.

Click here for Sonja's wonderful book, "The How of Happiness."

This begs the question: what do you think most people say would bring them more happiness? If you answered, "lots of money" you would be right.

Researcher Phil Brickman, however, discovered that ironically, a huge windfall does not create long-term happiness. Short-term? Yes. Long-term, no.

Larry David, the co-writer of *Seinfeld* and star of *Curb Your Enthusiasm* was once asked about how it felt being worth millions of dollars.

He answered, "Before *Seinfeld* I had problems such as paying the rent and putting food on the table. However, once I got a million dollars, these problems went away and overnight a new set of problems replaced them, such as 'What if I run out of all this money? Is the security at this building good enough? What if I get mugged just because I am wearing a particular watch? Are my friends laughing at my jokes because they think the jokes are funny, or just because I have lots of money?"

Interestingly, Brickman's researchers discovered that people who had won a lottery were no happier than a control group consisting of folks randomly selected from an Illinois telephone directory. The only difference between the two groups was that the folks in the phonebook group enjoyed the simple things of life more: sharing a joke online, receiving a compliment or enjoying a home-cooked meal.

Apparently most people adjust to having new things very quickly. Have you ever purchased a new car?

It may provide a short-term ego boost, but then after the novelty wears out, it just becomes a vehicle to transport you somewhere.

Likewise, once you receive a large sum of money, you get used to it quickly too. La-di-da. I've got millions of dollars. Big deal. It's like having a big tank full of water.

So if money isn't the best route to happiness, is there something else that might be? Yes. According to researchers, doing "random acts of kindness" increases the "giver's" happiness.

Doing unexpected things for other people without wanting anything in return will not only make you feel happy but like a row of dominoes, when you see others happy, you will not only feel happy but more successful.

The more successful you are, the more others may talk, tweet or text about you.

So if you belong to the prevailing culture of the Me Generation who like the sun impacts everything in its orbit, why not consider doing some random acts of kindness?

By the way, if you think I have been unfairly demonizing Millennials and that the description of GenMe doesn't fit you or anyone else you know, that's fine. Again my purpose in writing this book is **to increase your odds** for making a sale and not to describe the Me Generation perfectly. As mentioned, not every Millennial will have a tattoo or possess a body piercing.

Similarly, most GenMe'ers today believe that people should vote their passions not their pocketbooks. I think this attitude may change come 2016. Terrorism and its effects on the global economy as well as inflation and how it ultimately impacts an individual's pocketbook may cause many GenMe'ers to change their voting habits.

Therefore I am willing to make a bold prediction: if the Republican Party becomes less accommodating towards minorities, women's issues, and gay rights, it would not surprise me if Republicans win big in 2016. In fact, a familiar name may become the next US president.

With his Hispanic wife, an Iraqi daughter-in-law, and experience in leadership from having governed the state of Florida, I think GenMe'ers will probably find Jeb Bush an attractive presidential candidate. Why? Because I am some kind of ~~sick~~, whacko, conservative, nut-job?

Nope. It's just that the 12 psychological triggers for persuasion mentioned in this book strongly favor Jeb Bush.

Now don't be a hater.

I am just making a personal observation. Jeb Bush possesses more weapons of influence than any other Republican candidate.

A while ago I made a bold prediction about how I believed President Obama was going to win big in November 2012. Unfortunately, this book wasn't ready yet and my big prediction fizzled out like day-old soda.

So you might be wondering, how can this be?

Currently the right wing is in disarray from the 2012 election but remember: on the Internet, what exists today will probably exist differently tomorrow. Four years is practically a lifetime to a Me Generation voter, and a lot can happen during this time, but my prediction stands: Jeb Bush could win the 2016 election if he chooses to enter the race, targets GenMe voters, frames a strong "reason why" message and perhaps selects a GenMe'er as a Vice Presidential running mate. Who? I have no idea.

What about Hillary Clinton? Yes, she too wields enormous influence. The problem she has concerning GenMe voters is that they are a contrarian and individualistic bunch. I think a large majority of GenMe will change from being a "vote with your passion gang" into a "vote with your pocketbook" bunch. That's all I'm going to say for right now. Again, I am a Klutz too so I could be completely wrong. This is just my observation.

Be aware too that the individualist spirit of Generation Me isn't all bad. I think that a proud and shining moment for Millennials occurred in 2012 after the summer Olympic games.

That's right, AFTER the London Olympics were over; the 2012 Paralympic Games were also celebrated in London.

These games honor men and women whom Baby Boomers and The Greatest Generation would probably never consider to be worthy of being acknowledged in an Olympic venue because they are physically challenged.

Yet members of GenMe warmed up to these individual athletes and attended the Paralympics in large numbers. The idiosyncratic spirit of the Me Generation showed the world that physically challenged people are important members of our society too. So please don't be too critical of Generation Me. They may not all invent Facebook, but give them time, space and room to fly and you might be surprised at what they can do.

This brings me now to **The Lucky Coconut Story**.

One evening my wife called to tell me that we were out of milk at home. She asked, "Would you mind visiting the grocery store on your way home from work?" So later that night, I stopped by Vons and after I picked up the ~~six cartons of~~ milk and one avocado that she had requested, I decided to check out the bananas. My mother-in-law, Clemen, lives with us, and because she likes to put bananas on her cereal for breakfast, I decided to surprise her by purchasing a bunch of fresh bananas.

Then I encountered a bit of trouble. Not sure if this has ever happened to you, but I could not for the life of me figure out which side of the static-charged, ultra-thin, plastic bag I was supposed to open in order to put the fruit inside.

I am near-sighted so I had to remove my glasses and surgically inspect each side of the plastic.

Once I succeeded in correctly opening it, and dutifully dropping the bananas into the plastic bag; I then couldn't locate my glasses.

Have you ever tried to find your specs when you don't have your spectacles on? Not fun.

Fortunately, I found my eyeglasses because I had set them atop some nearby coconuts.

Most of the coconuts came wrapped in plastic, but a few of them weren't. They were exposed to the great unwashed public. That's then when I made another one of my famous observations.

Wow. Coconuts are really hairy to the touch!

Have you ever noticed this? I actually picked one up and marveled at its weight and the unique texture of the coconut. It's truly amazing!

I had never really noticed this furry texture before, but I realized: Wow, this is so cool. I have got to buy this hairy coconut and give it to my wife!

So that's what I did. I purchased the ~~six cartons of~~ milk, avocado, bananas and the coconut and left the store.

That night I gave the bananas to my mother-in-law but I hid the coconut from my wife. My wife works with me so I thought I would surprise her with it.

The next day, I made a little handwritten card and left it on her desk with the coconut. My card announced that I had found a "Lucky Coconut" that could grant her every wish. She just had to rub its hairy head. I wrote that not only would it **guarantee** that we would make millions of dollars with it, but it would personally cheer her up and make her day more wonderful.

Did the lucky coconut help us make more money?

No, I can't say that it did.

Did it cheer up my wife and make her smile that morning? Yes, it certainly did. She even picked up a black sharpie pen and immediately drew two eyes and a big smile on it.

(Why didn't I think of that?)

Did the lucky coconut help me get lucky that night? Um, I'll let you guess! ;-)

Did the lucky coconut with the smiling face make me happier that morning?

Yes it did, because when you see someone close to you smiling, and telling you sweet things like "You are just so weird" and watching her enjoy her goofy-looking coconut, you would probably smile too. Now if you do this please note that a coconut is only good for a couple of weeks! After that it starts to reek to high heaven. It may attract ants too, if you leave it unattended long enough!

The moral of this story is that sometimes it's good to **surrender to serendipity.**

Something good or useful can appear when you are not specifically searching for it.

Be spontaneous. Tap your intuition. Test new insights. Follow your hunches and chase down your efforts. Lucky coconuts are all around us – you just have to notice them. And when you do, take action.

Obviously you will want to analyze all possible blind spots, but if it's appropriate, move ahead. Perhaps you've been toying with the idea of buying a Harley, or changing careers, or entering a new exciting field or even acquiring a new business.

If you have analyzed all the angles and things look good, take a chance and surrender to serendipity.

Maybe it's something as simple as trying out one of these psychological cues but adding your own twist.

Yes there may be risks involved but there may be unanticipated benefits too. Your new endeavor may bring about unexpected windfalls that you had not considered.

You might even have more fun too.

What a concept!

Look, we all know that selling is a job. And every job is about making money; yet no job is really about money, is it? Jobs are also about building and maintaining relationships with people and the things you do in this little square we call life.

Yet isn't life about having fun and putting love into what you are doing – even if sometimes you have to hold your nose and smile while you're doing it?

In other words, sometimes you have to make up reasons to feel good before those feel-good feelings start flowing. So realize that sometimes you have to fake it before you make it. You may find that optimism, even of the irrational variety can still be serotonin producing.

There's also an old saying that goes, "if you aren't having any fun, then you must be doing something wrong."

So look for ways to have more fun and put more passion into your life and what you do. My friend, there are a lot of people who would give their right arm to be able to work again but cannot do so. Work is a great privilege. Treat it like the enormous opportunity it is. If you have been feeling down lately or complaining about your job, the economy, higher taxes or whatever – go to a grocery store and buy someone a lucky coconut.

Seriously, fake cheerfulness or try to make someone else smile.

Find a way to make your job more fun.

Express an attitude of gratitude not only for your job, but for your country, your freedom, your health and for the well-being and good cheer of those who work with you.

English novelist Douglas Adams once wrote, "To give real service you must add something which cannot be bought or measured with money. That is sincerity and integrity."

If you are in business for the long run, ask yourself if that is what you are doing. **Am I offering sincerity and integrity to my customers?**

If not, can you start doing so from now on and have fun doing it?

Well, I have to admit. I have had a lot of fun talking about my favorite subject: ~~me~~ selling.

But this marks the end of this book. I sincerely appreciate that you took your valuable time today to read it. If you enjoyed it, I would be grateful if you tweeted or left a review about it on the website, or Facebook or Amazon or even just recommended it to a friend, but that's not required. I write books mainly because I ~~need money~~ have fun doing so.

If you didn't like this book, ~~tough luck~~ no problem, just shoot me an email of what you didn't like. Use the email at the website www.sellingoutsidethesquare.com and I will keep your comments confidential but take them to heart when I rewrite the book. There are also resources, ideas, possibly videos and other material at the website, so please check it out.

Now in my family when it's time to say goodbye, I will personally extend my hand and shake yours. Or I will step towards you and give you a hug. If you are a special female in my life, I may even kiss you on the cheek while giving you a hug. It's with that same feeling of love and appreciation that I extend to you now.

Warmest personal regards,

Bob Boog
Valencia, California

Seven Creative Thinking Questions

Now since the book is over, I can share with you a simple observation that I made because it will help me to slide into this after-the-book-is-over section about creative thinking. My observation was nothing earth shattering, in fact, I just want you to look at a common object slightly differently than maybe you had before. Here is how it came about:

My wife and I took a week's vacation with five other families at Bass Lake, CA. We slept in different cabins and each night, one of the families hosted a themed dinner party. Everyone had to dress up in costumes to match the theme. Monday night, for example was Mexican night. One family cooked a Mexican dinner for everybody, and we wore Mexican costumes, and drank Coronas. There was a Toga night where we ate Mediterranean food and even a Redneck themed party where we cooked hot dogs and ate spam. It was a lot of fun and best of all my wife only had to cook dinner one night of the week. She loved that part!

By chance, when I was laying newspapers on the picnic table (to create a Redneck table cloth) I happened to notice a "Fugitives Wanted by the Police" article in the local newspaper. The half-page article featured pictures and descriptions of dangerous fugitives who were wanted by law enforcement because of the crimes they had committed. True story.

To me the people in the newspaper looked like some REAL low-life rednecks.

So I snapped a digital picture of the newspaper and then later, after the vacation was over, for a bit of skullduggery I photo-shopped the faces of my friends dressed up like Rednecks and merged them with the real life newspaper article.

Later, I started hanging around with the idea that maybe this Redneck idea could make a cool Facebook app. Perhaps I could call it "Redneck Mug Shot!"

Here is how it would work.

Using a cell phone, a person could take a head shot; upload the picture to the Facebook Redneck Mug Shot app and it would then create a humorous "redneck" profile.

Perhaps the finished product would give you a new funny Redneck name with a crime to boot.

Nothing earth shattering, but fun, right? Do you think people might use an app like this on Facebook to play a joke on a friend? Maybe yes, maybe no.

Then I got to thinking, what if I could make an app for a book called *Selling Outside the Square*? Anyway, I digress. The point of this story is that it got me thinking about a familiar object in a different way. So come along with me now. I want to share my thought process with you. I want you to look beyond something obvious and imagine it with a different perspective.

Just for a minute, I want you to stop your shenanigans and imagine that you are a seven year old child once again. Let your imagination run wild. I want you to think about a device from the fantastic future. This device can be used:

As a movie camera	*Push a button it's an alarm clock*
It's a calculator	*Press a button and it's a camera*
You can view a map	*Input earphones to hear music*
You can watch TV on it	*It can even scan documents*
It's got a flashlight & a compass and a camcorder!	*Send messages to friends*

This device can even make phone calls!

Cool device, isn't it? Doesn't it sound like something James Bond or The Man from U.N.C.L.E. might have? What's it called? I call it my iPhone, but it can be just about any smart device.

Now, how does describing the features of an iPhone like it's a fantasy object relate to selling outside the square?

While thinking about fantasy ideas concerning my iPhone I mentioned to a friend "Wouldn't it be cool if I could press a button on my cell phone and it could stop a dog in its tracks? He just started to laugh. I continued.

"This way if I entered a house I could stop the dog from attacking me." (In real estate, some folks make it difficult to show a home because they leave their dogs inside the house.) Maybe my magical device could even bark LOUD like a pit-bull and that might scare off another dog."

My friend finally said, "Bob, your idea about barking like a dog reminded me of something you would probably really get into. It's called the TRIZ project and it's basically about how engineers use a pattern for creative problem solving. Actually they are using computer algorhythms."

To make a long story short, some computer engineers made a list of how to creatively solve problems then boiled it down into various principles. After reading about these creative problem-solving laws, I turned them into seven questions to make them easier to read.

It is my pleasure to share these seven questions and 40+ corollaries compliments of www.TRIZ-journal.com with you. I love the brain-storming answers to this material but if it doesn't interest you, skip it and view the jokes on page 114. Or skip that too and the book is over!

1. The Segmentation Question: Can the object be divided into different parts?

Divide an object into independent parts
-Replace mainframe computer by personal computers.
-Replace a large truck by a truck and trailer.
-Use a work breakdown structure for a large project.
Make an object easy to disassemble
-Quick disconnects joints in plumbing. Modular furniture
-Replace solid shades with Venetian blinds.
-Use powdered welding metal instead of foil or rod to get better penetration of the joint.
Increase the degree of fragmentation or segmentation
-Locate a noisy compressor outside the building where compressed air is used.
-Use fiber optics or a light pipe to separate the hot light source from the location where light is needed.
-Use the sound of a barking dog, without the dog, as a burglar alarm

2. The Changeability Question: Can something be added to the object?

Change an object's structure from uniform to non-uniform, change an external environment (or external influence) from uniform to non-uniform.
- Use a temperature, density, or pressure gradient instead of constant temperature, density or pressure.
Make each part of an object function in conditions most suitable for its operation.
- Lunch box with special compartments for hot and cold solid foods and for liquids.

Make each part of an object fulfill a different and useful function.
- Pencil with eraser
- Hammer with nail puller
- Multi-function tool that scales fish, acts as a pliers, a wire stripper, a flat-blade screwdriver, a Phillips screwdriver, manicure set, etc.

Change the shape of an object from symmetrical to asymmetrical.
- Asymmetrical mixing vessels or asymmetrical vanes in symmetrical vessels improve mixing (cement trucks, cake mixers, blenders).
- Put a flat spot on a cylindrical shaft to attach a knob securely. If an object is asymmetrical, increase its degree of asymmetry.
- Change from circular O-rings to oval cross-section to specialized shapes to improve sealing.
- Use astigmatic optics to merge colors.

Bring closer together (or merge) identical or similar objects, assemble identical or similar parts to perform parallel operations.
- Personal computers in a network
- Thousands of microprocessors in a parallel processor computer
- Vanes in a ventilation system
- Electronic chips mounted on both sides of a circuit board or subassembly

Make operations contiguous or parallel; bring them together in time.
- Link slats together in Venetian or vertical blinds.
- Medical diagnostic instruments that analyze multiple blood parameters simultaneously
- Mulching lawnmower

Make a part or object perform multiple functions; eliminate the need for other parts.
Handle of a toothbrush contains toothpaste
Child s car safety seat converts to a stroller

Mulching lawnmower (Yes, it demonstrates both Principles 5 and 6, Merging and Universality.)
Team leader acts as recorder and timekeeper.
CCD (Charge coupled device) with micro-lenses formed on the surface

Place one object inside another; place each object, in turn, inside the other.
- Measuring cups or spoons
- Russian dolls
- Portable audio system (microphone fits inside transmitter, which fits inside amplifier case)

Make one part pass through a cavity in the other.
- Extending radio antenna
- Extending pointer
- Zoom lens
- Seat belt retraction mechanism
- Retractable aircraft landing

3. The Preliminary Action or Anti-Action Question:
Can an action or anti-action be added?

In Los Angeles, the freeway was closed so that a concrete bridge that spanned the 405 freeway could be felled on Carmageddon day. After contractors cut the bridge, a huge swath of concrete crashed onto the lanes of the concrete freeway below.

Question: What did the contracting company do to avoid destroying the existing concrete freeway below?

Answer: The contractor made a mountain of sand to cushion the fall of the bridge, and then later hauled all the sand and chunks of concrete away.

If it will be necessary to do an action with both harmful and useful effects, this action should be replaced with anti-actions to control harmful effects.

- Buffer a solution to prevent harm from extremes of pH.
Create beforehand stresses in an object that will oppose known undesirable working stresses later on.
- Pre-stress rebar before pouring concrete.
- Masking anything before harmful exposure: Use a lead apron on parts of the body not being exposed to X-rays. Use masking tape to protect the part of an object not being painted

Perform, before it is needed, the required change of an object (either fully or partially).
- Pre-pasted wall paper
- Sterilize all instruments needed for a surgical procedure on a sealed tray.
Pre-arrange objects such that they can come into action from the most convenient place and without losing time for their delivery.
- Kanab arrangements in a Just-In-Time factory
- Flexible manufacturing cell

Prepare emergency means beforehand to compensate for the relatively low reliability of an object.
- Magnetic strip on photographic film that directs the developer to compensate for poor exposure
- Back-up parachute
- Alternate air system for aircraft instruments

In a potential field, limit position changes (e.g. change operating conditions to eliminate the need to raise or lower objects in a gravity field).

- Spring loaded parts delivery system in a factory
- Locks in a channel between 2 bodies of water (Panama Canal)
- Skillets in an automobile plant that bring all tools to the right position

4. The Other Way Around Question: Can an opposite approach be used?

Invert the action(s) used to solve the problem (e.g. instead of cooling an object, heat it).

- To loosen stuck parts, cool the inner part instead of heating the outer part.
- **Bring the mountain to Mohammed, instead of bringing Mohammed to the mountain.**

Make movable parts (or the external environment) fixed, and fixed parts movable.

- Rotate the part instead of the tool.
- Moving sidewalk with standing people.
- Treadmill (for walking or running in place.)

Turn the object (or process) 'upside down'.

- Turn an assembly upside down to insert fasteners (especially screws).
- Empty grain from containers (ship or railroad) by inverting them.

Instead of using rectilinear parts, surfaces, or forms, use curvilinear ones; move from flat surfaces to spherical ones; from parts shaped as a cube (parallelepiped) to ball-shaped structures.

Use arches and domes for strength in architecture.
Use rollers, balls, spirals, and domes.
- Spiral gear (Nautilus) produces continuous resistance for weight lifting.
- Ballpoint and roller point pens for smooth ink distribution
Go from linear to rotary motion, use centrifugal forces.
- Produce linear motion of the cursor on the computer screen using a mouse or a trackball.
- Replace wringing clothes to remove water with spinning clothes in a washing machine.
- Use spherical casters instead of cylindrical wheels to move furniture.

Allow (or design) the characteristics of an object, external environment, or process to change to be optimal or to find an optimal operating condition.
- Adjustable steering wheel (or seat, or back support, or mirror position...)
Divide an object into parts capable of movement relative to each other.
- The *butterfly* computer keyboard, (also demonstrates Principle 7, *Nested doll*.)
If an object (or process) is rigid or inflexible, make it movable or adaptive.
- The flexible baroscopic for examining engines
- The flexible sigmoid-scope, for medical examination

If 100 percent of an object is hard to achieve using a given solution method then, by using 'slightly less' or 'slightly more' of the same method, the problem may be considerably easier to solve.

- Over spray when painting, then remove excess. (Or, use a stencil--this is an application of Principle 3, Local Quality and Principle 9, Preliminary anti-action).
- Fill, then *top off* when filling the gas tank of your car.

5. The Dimensions and Vibrations Question: Can the object be rearranged dimensionally and/or vibrated?

Change dimensions of an object or move an object in two- or three-dimensional space.
- Infrared computer mouse moves in space, instead of on a surface, for presentations.

- Five-axis cutting tool can be positioned where needed.

Use a multi-story arrangement of objects instead of a single-story arrangement.

- Cassette with 6 CD s to increase music time and variety
- Electronic chips on both sides of a printed circuit board
- Employees *disappear* from the customers in a theme park, descend into a tunnel, and walk to their next assignment, where they return to the surface and magically reappear.
Tilt or re-orient the object, lay it on its side.
- Dump truck
Use 'another side' of a given area.
- Stack microelectronic hybrid circuits to improve density.

Cause an object to oscillate or vibrate.
- Electric carving knife with vibrating blades
Increase its frequency (even up to the ultrasonic).
- Distribute powder with vibration.

Use an object's resonant frequency.
- Destroy gallstones or kidney stones using ultrasonic resonance.
Use piezoelectric vibrators instead of mechanical ones.
- Quartz crystal oscillations drive high accuracy clocks.
Use combined ultrasonic and electromagnetic field oscillations.
- Mixing alloys in an induction furnace

Instead of continuous action, use periodic or pulsating actions.
- Hitting something repeatedly with a hammer
- Replace a continuous siren with a pulsed sound.

If an action is already periodic, change the periodic magnitude or frequency.
- Use Frequency Modulation to convey information, instead of Morse code.
- Replace a continuous siren with sound that changes amplitude and frequency.
Use pauses between impulses to perform a different action.
- In cardio-pulmonary respiration (CPR) breathe after every 5-chest compressions.

Carry on work continuously; make all parts of an object work at full load, all the time.
- Flywheel (or hydraulic system) stores energy when a vehicle stops, so the motor can keep running at optimum power.
- Run the bottleneck operations in a factory continuously, to reach the optimum pace. (From theory of constraints, or take the time operations)

Eliminate all idle or intermittent actions or work.
- Print during the return of a printer carriage--dot matrix printer, daisy wheel printers, and inkjet printers.

Conduct a process, or certain stages (e.g. destructible, harmful or hazardous operations) at high speed.
- Use a high-speed dentist s drill to avoid heating tissue.
- Cut plastic faster than heat can propagate in the material, to avoid deforming the shape.

6. Turning Lemons into Lemonade Question:
Can harmful effects be used to create a positive effect?

Use harmful factors (particularly, harmful effects of the environment or surroundings) to achieve a positive effect.
- Use waste heat to generate electric power.
- Recycle waste (scrap) material from one process as raw materials for another.

Eliminate the primary harmful action by adding it to another harmful action to resolve the problem.
- Add a buffering material to a corrosive solution.
- Use a helium-oxygen mix for diving, to eliminate both nitrogen narcosis and oxygen poisoning from air and other nitrox mixes.
Amplify a harmful factor to such a degree that it is no longer harmful.
- Use a backfire to eliminate the fuel from a forest fire.

Introduce feedback (referring back, cross-checking) to improve a process or action.
- Automatic volume control in audio circuits
- Signal from gyrocompass is used to control simple aircraft autopilots.

- Statistical Process Control (SPC) -- Measurements are used to decide when to modify a process. (Not all feedback systems are automated!)
- Budgets --Measurements are used to decide when to modify a process.

If feedback is already used, change its magnitude or influence.

- Change sensitivity of an autopilot when within 5 miles of an airport.
- Change sensitivity of a thermostat when cooling vs. heating, since it uses energy less efficiently when cooling.
- Change a management measure from budget variance to customer satisfaction.

Use an intermediary carrier article or intermediary process.

- Carpenters nail set, used between the hammer and the nail Merge one object temporarily with another (which can be easily removed).
- Use a potholder to carry hot dishes to the table

Make an object serve itself by performing auxiliary helpful functions

- A soda fountain pump that runs on the pressure of the carbon dioxide that is used to *fizz* the drinks. This assures that drinks will not be flat, and eliminates the need for sensors.

- Halogen lamps regenerate the filament during use-- evaporated material is re-deposited.
- To weld steel to aluminum, create an interface from alternating thin strips of the 2 materials. Cold weld the surface into a single unit with steel on one face and copper on the other, then use normal welding techniques to attach the steel object to the interface, and the interface to the aluminum

Use waste resources, energy, or substances.
- Use heat from a process to generate electricity: *Co-generation*.
- Use animal waste as fertilizer.
- Use food and lawn waste to create compost.

Instead of an unavailable, expensive, fragile object, use simpler and inexpensive copies.
- Virtual reality via computer instead of an expensive vacation
- Listen to an audiotape instead of attending a seminar.
Replace an object, or process with optical copies.
- Do surveying from space photographs instead of on the ground.
- Measure an object by measuring the photograph.
- Make sonograms to evaluate the health of a fetus, instead of risking damage by direct testing.
If visible optical copies are already used, move to infrared or ultraviolet copies.
- Make images in infrared to detect heat sources, such as diseases in crops, or intruders in a security system.

Replace an inexpensive object with a multiple of inexpensive objects, comprising certain qualities (such as service life, for instance).

- Use disposable paper objects to avoid the cost of cleaning and storing durable objects. Plastic cups in motels, disposable diapers, many kinds of medical supplies.

7. The Changing States Question: Can the properties of the object be altered?

Make an object porous or add porous elements (inserts, coatings, etc.).
- Drill holes in a structure to reduce the weight.
If an object is already porous, use the pores to introduce a useful substance or function.
- Use a porous metal mesh to wick excess solder away from a joint.
- Store hydrogen in the pores of a palladium sponge. (Fuel *tank* for the hydrogen car--much safer than storing hydrogen gas)

Change the color of an object or its external environment.
- Use safe lights in a photographic darkroom.
Replace a mechanical means with a sensory (optical, acoustic, taste or smell) means.
- Replace a physical fence to confine a dog or cat with an acoustic *fence* (signal audible to the animal).
- Use a bad smelling compound in natural gas to alert users to leakage, instead of a mechanical or electrical sensor.

Use electric, magnetic and electromagnetic fields to interact with the object.
- To mix 2 powders, electro-statically charge one positive and the other negative. Either use fields to direct them, or mix them mechanically and let their acquired fields cause the grains of powder to pair up.

Change from static to movable fields, from unstructured fields to those having structure.
- Early communications used omni-directional broadcasting. We now use antennas with very detailed structure of the pattern of radiation.

Use fields in conjunction with field-activated (e.g. ferromagnetic) particles.
- Heat a substance containing ferromagnetic material by using varying magnetic field. When the temperature exceeds the Curie point, the material becomes paramagnetic, and no longer absorbs heat.

Use gas and liquid parts of an object instead of solid parts (e.g. inflatable, filled with liquids, air cushion, hydrostatic, hydro-reactive).
- Comfortable shoe sole inserts filled with gel
- Store energy from decelerating a vehicle in a hydraulic system, then use the stored energy to accelerate later.

Use flexible shells and thin films instead of three-dimensional structures
- Use inflatable (thin film) structures as winter covers on tennis courts.
Isolate the object from the external environment using flexible shells and thin films.
- Float a film of bipolar material (one end hydrophilic, one end hydrophobic) on a reservoir to limit evaporation.

Change the transparency of an object or its external environment.
- Use photo-lithography to change transparent material to a solid mask for semiconductor processing. Similarly, change mask material from transparent to opaque for silkscreen processing.

Make objects interacting with a given object of the same material (or material with identical properties).
- Make the container out of the same material as the contents, to reduce chemical reactions.
- Make a diamond-cutting tool out of diamonds.

Make portions of an object that have fulfilled their functions go away (discard by dissolving, evaporating, etc.) or modify these directly during operation.
- Use a dissolving capsule for medicine.
- Sprinkle water on cornstarch-based packaging and watch it reduce its volume by more than 1000X!

- Ice structures: use water ice or carbon dioxide (dry ice) to make a template for a rammed earth structure, such as a temporary dam. Fill with earth, then, let the ice melt or sublime to leave the final structure.
Conversely, restore consumable parts of an object directly in operation.

- Self-sharpening lawn mower blades
- Automobile engines that give themselves a *tune up* while running (the ones that say *100,000 miles between tune ups*)

Change an object's physical state (e.g. to a gas, liquid, or solid.)
- Freeze the liquid centers of filled candies, and then dip in melted chocolate, instead of handling the messy, gooey, hot liquid.
- Transport oxygen or nitrogen or petroleum gas as a liquid, instead of a gas, to reduce volume.

Change the concentration or consistency.
Liquid hand soap is concentrated and more viscous than bar soap at the point of use, making it easier to dispense in the correct amount and more sanitary when shared by several people.

Change the degree of flexibility.
- Use adjustable dampers to reduce the noise of parts falling into a container by restricting the motion of the walls of the container.
- Vulcanize rubber to change its flexibility and durability.

Change the temperature.
- Raise the temperature above the Curie point to change a ferromagnetic substance to a paramagnetic substance.
- Raise the temperature of food to cook it. (Changes taste, aroma, texture, chemical properties, etc.)
- Lower the temperature of medical specimens to preserve them for later analysis.

Use phenomena occurring during phase transitions (e.g. volume changes, loss or absorption of heat, etc.).
- Water expands when frozen, unlike most other liquids
 Hannibal is reputed to have used this when marching on Rome a few thousand years ago. Large rocks blocked passages in the Alps. He poured water on them at night. The overnight cold froze the water, and the expansion split the rocks into small pieces, which could be pushed aside.
- Heat pumps use the heat of vaporization and heat of condensation of a closed thermodynamic cycle to do useful work.

Use thermal expansion (or contraction) of materials.
- Fit a tight joint together by cooling the inner part to contract, heating the outer part to expand, putting the joint together, and returning to equilibrium.
If thermal expansion is being used, use multiple materials with different coefficients of thermal expansion.
- The basic leaf spring thermostat: (2 metals with different coefficients of expansion are linked so that it bends one way when warmer than nominal and the opposite way when cooler.)

Replace common air with oxygen-enriched air.
- Scuba diving with Nitrox or other non-air mixtures for extended endurance
Replace enriched air with pure oxygen.

Cut at a higher temperature using an oxy-acetylene torch.
- Treat wounds in a high-pressure oxygen environment to kill anaerobic bacteria and aid healing.

Replace a normal environment with an inert one.
- Prevent degradation of a hot metal filament by using an argon atmosphere.
Add neutral parts, or inert additives to an object.
- Increase the volume of powdered detergent by adding inert ingredients. This makes it easier to measure with conventional tools.

Change from uniform to composite (multiple) materials.
- Composite epoxy resin/carbon fiber golf club shafts are lighter, stronger, and more flexible than metal. Same for airplane parts.
- Fiberglass surfboards are lighter and more controllable and easier to form into a variety of shapes than wooden ones.

Selling Outside the Square Humor

Q. How can you drop a raw egg onto a concrete floor without cracking it?
A. Concrete floors are very hard to crack!

Q. If it took eight men ten hours to build a wall, how long would it take four men to build it?
A. No time at all since it is already built.

Q. If you had three apples and four oranges in one hand and four apples and three oranges in the other hand, what would you have?
A. Very large hands.

Q. How can you lift an elephant with one hand?
A. It is not a problem, since you will never find an elephant with one hand.

Q. How can a man go eight days without sleep?
A. It's no problem because he sleeps at night.

Q. If you throw a red stone into the blue sea what it will become?
A. It will become wet and sink; it's as simple as that.

Q. What looks like half an apple ?
A : The other half.

Q. What can you never eat for breakfast ?
A : Lunch and dinner.

Five Laws for Selling Outside the Square

1. The Law of Two Heads are Better than One

- Ask for help from someone who doesn't have a personal or technical involvement in your problem or situation

- Ask your "better half"

- Ask the universe, God, Spirit or Mother Nature for help

- Ask a child, teenager or senior for assistance

2. The Law of Relaxation

- Take a bath or shower to help free your mind

- Visit a museum, look at great art

- Take a walk, walk barefoot on the grass

- Dig the earth with your fingers, smell flowers, pick weeds or prune your garden

- Meditate outside and listen to the birds

- Read a book

- Take a nap

- Watch cartoons

3. The Law of Changing into Something Else

- Study another industry similar to yours- but not yours.

- Study another religion

- Write a poem about your problem, and try to use a metaphor to describe it

> ➢ Draw your problem, paint something else that feels like it

> ➢ Sing your problem, sing feelings about it

> ➢ Type a similar phrase into Google, but make it slightly different

> ➢ Fake it. Act like you know it already, write the processes that person would do

4 The Law of Starting from the End

- Re-imagine the story with the end being the starting point and move backward to the beginning

- Turn it upside down

- Flip it, imagine if it was happening to you

- Turn it over or sideways, there may be patterns you didn't see before

- Change the orientation of an object. Change your orientation

5. The Law of Taking Massive Actions

- Take a class, find out more info on YouTube or Google

- Be brave and courageous

- Listen to others, don't be auto-dismissive

- Step on toes only if needed to be persistent

- Don't take no for an answer

- Send handwritten thank you notes OFTEN

Helpful Resources

Generation Me: Why Today's Young Americans Are More Confident, Assertive, Entitled and More Miserable Than Ever Before by Jean M. Twenge, Ph.D. Free Press, A Division of Simon & Schuster, Inc. 2006

Influence: The Psychology of Persuasion, by Robert B. Ciladini, PH.D.
Quill, William Morrow, New York, ©1984 and 1993.

59 Seconds Change Your Life in Under a Minute by Richard Wiseman Anchor Books, NY © 2011

The Power of Habit: Why We Do What We Do In Life And Business by Charles Duhigg, Random House, New York © 2011

The Purpose Driven Life, Scriptures for the Graduate by Rick Warren, Inspirio © 2004 the gift group of Zondervan, Grand Rapids, MI

You Are What You Love by Vaishali, © 2006 Purple Haze Books – a wonderful book about love and you.

Other Books by Bob Boog

Real Estate Sales from Hell
Selling Homes 1-2-3
Mortgage Modifications Made Easy
Urgent, by Roberto Palomo (www.urgent-book.com)

Index

A

Alka Seltzer, 59

American Idol, 38,,57,67

B

Baby Boomers, 14-16, 111

Bass Lake, 82

Bible, 8

C

Celebrity, 66-67

Changeability,6, 86

Changing States, 6,97

Columbo, 69-70

commitment, 5, 49-52,56

cookie experiment, 54

Costco, 59,62

Craigslist, 80

Curiosity 5, 45-47

D

Dennis Regan, 62

Dimensions and Vibrations, 6,92

F

Facebook, 21,38,42,48,61,70-71,73,76-77,83,111,115

Feel, felt, found, 42-43

Freedman and Fraser, 50

G

Generation Me, 17- 23,25,28, 32, 37-40,44-45,47,51-52,54-56,59-61,64,67-72,76,80,109-110

Gordon Ramsay, 47

Great-Grandma Effect, 24

H

happiness then success, 107

Humor, 7,37,83,103

I

iPhone, 52,84

J

Johnny Walker, 59-60

K

Kohl's, 78

L

Larry David, 105

Law of Changing into Something, 116

Law of Relaxation, 115

Law of Rewarding Self after Doing, 117

Law of Starting from the End, 116

Law of Massive Action, 117

Law of Two Heads, 115

LeBron James, 75-76

Lender, 9, 72,87

Lucky Coconut, 88-92

M

Maureen Stout, 68

McDonald's,9,75,78

mortgage meltdown, 7,57 63

N

Nicolas Gueguen, 42

O

Obama,20,109

Objections, 40

Observation, ,29-30,35,37,42,61,81,109,111

Other Way Around, 6,90

P

Paralympic Games, 109

Playboy Magazine, 60

Politics, 20,73

Preliminary Action, 6,88

R

random acts of kindness, 107-108

Reciprocation, 6, 62

Redneck, 82-83

Robert Cialdini Ph.D, 25

S

Sanka, 66,71

Scarcity, 5, 52-55

Segmentation, 6,85-86

sending emails, 38,51

smart device, 79,84

social proof, 57-61,79

Sonja Lyubomirsky, 106

Stories, 28, 32-36

Story about Wise Man, 33,37

Story about Mountain, 34-35

Story with email, 36-37

Summer Olympics, 75

T

Tell the truth, 79

The Wizard of Oz, 8

Tom Hopkins, 29, 48

Touch, 42-43,111

TRIZ, 85

Turning Lemons into Lemonade, 94

Twenge, Jean M.,16-17

Twitter, 20,47,70

W

What About Bob, 48

Wikipedia, 21

Will Rogers, 52

William Hung, 30,57

www.mailchimp.com, 52

www.TextInfotoClient.com, 27

Y

YouTube, 18,41,61,71,77,104

www.ingramcontent.com/pod-product-compliance
Lightning Source LLC
Chambersburg PA
CBHW060618210326
41520CB00010B/1389